★ FACTS AMERICA

DINOSAURS

MICHAEL BENTON AND ELLEN WEISS

SMITHMARK

About the authors

Michael Benton, lecturer in paleontology at the University of Bristol, England, has loved dinosaurs since he was seven. He has written 14 books on dinosaurs and other aspects of the history of life. Dr. Benton has worked on scientific problems concerning the origin of dinosaurs, their evolution, and extinction. He is currently working on new finds of fossil reptiles, including dinosaurs, in England and Scotland.

Ellen Weiss, a children's writer since 1972, has published more than 50 books and many science articles, and has also written television shows and videos for children. Ms. Weiss has received the Children's Choice Award three times. Her latest novel, *The Poof Point*, was written with her husband, Mel Friedman. She lives with him and their daughter, Nora, in New York City.

Editor:
Philip de Ste. Croix

Designer:
Stonecastle Graphics Ltd

Picture research:
Leora Kahn

Coordinating editors:
Andrew Preston
Kristen Schilo

Production:
Ruth Arthur
Sally Connolly
Neil Randles
Andrew Whitelaw

Production editor:
Didi Charney

Director of production:
Gerald Hughes

Typesetter:
Pagesetters Incorporated

Color and monochrome reproduction:
Advance Laser Graphic Arts, Hong Kong

Printed and bound in Hong Kong
by Leefung-Asco Printers Ltd

1992 Colour Library Books Ltd
Godalming Business Centre
Woolsack Way, Godalming
Surrey GU7 1XW, United Kingdom
CLB 2606

This edition published in 1992 by
SMITHMARK Publishers Inc.
112 Madison Avenue
New York, NY 10016 USA

SMITHMARK books are available
for bulk purchase for sales promotion
and premium use. For details, write or call the manager of special sales,
SMITHMARK Publishers Inc., 112 Madison Avenue, New York, NY 10016;
(212) 532-6600.

Library of Congress Cataloging-in-Publication Data

Benton, M. J. (Michael J.)
   Facts America. Dinosaurs / Michael Benton & Ellen Weiss.
      p.   cm.
   Includes bibliographical references and index.
   Summary: Discusses our knowledge of the dinosaurs and the fossil
evidence that supports it.
   ISBN 0-8317-2313-0 (hardcover)
   1. Dinosaurs—Juvenile literature.   2. Paleontology—Juvenile
literature.   [1. Dinosaurs.   2. Fossils.   3. Paleontology.]
I. Weiss, Ellen, 1949–   II. Title.   III. Title: Dinosaurs.
QE862.2.D5B465   1992
567.9′1—dc20   92-9462

Here are some of the fiercest dinosaurs that ever existed. These meat-eating giants are all tyrannosaurs; from left to right, we see Daspletosaurus, Tyrannosaurus, *and* Tarbosaurus. *A fully grown man would scarcely reach up to their knees.*

Contents

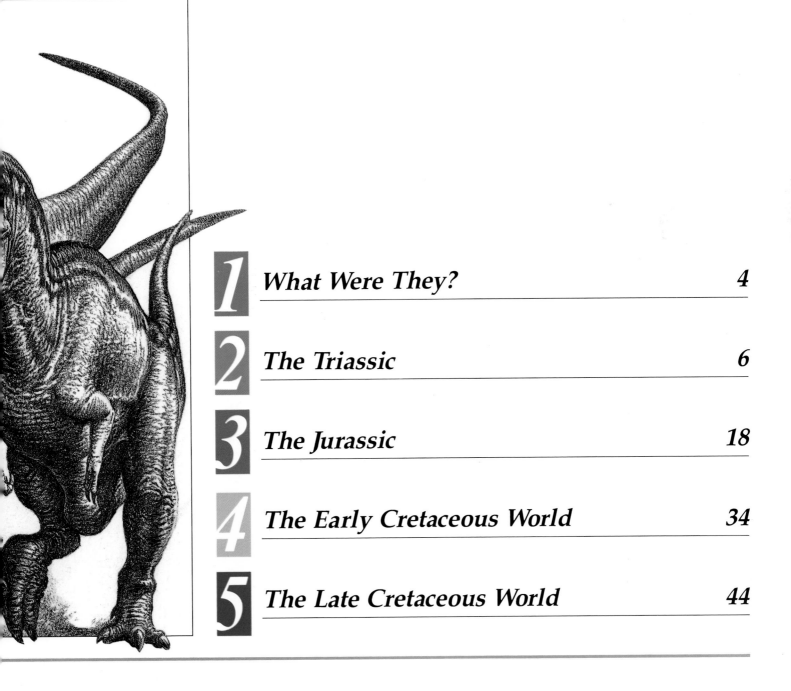

What Were They?

Many millions of years before humans appeared, the earth was ruled by dinosaurs. They came in all sizes and shapes: big ones, little ones, meat eaters, plant eaters, spiky ones, and smooth ones.

EARLY RELATIVES: Dinosaurs began appearing on earth about 230 million years ago, during the Mesozoic era, which is often called the Age of the Dinosaurs. Before this time, there were other animals on the planet. There were early amphibians, and there were also reptiles, which evolved, or changed over time, from amphibians. Many of these animals continued to exist along with the dinosaurs and kept on evolving after the dinosaurs died out.

Dinosaurs were themselves a group of reptiles that evolved from those early reptiles. What made the dinosaurs different were their legs. Instead of having short legs that splayed out from their bodies, like those of crocodiles, they had pillarlike legs that were right under their bodies. This got their bellies up off the ground. The dinosaurs' legs enabled some of them to grow very big and some of them to move very fast. Some could even walk on two legs.

BONING UP: Almost all we know about dinosaurs, we know from their bones. When a dinosaur died, often its bones would decay and disappear. But sometimes they would sink into the soft mud or silt at the bottom of a lake or sea. There, they would be covered up with more mud or silt, which formed layers of what is called sediment. Eventually, over millions of years, the sediment built up, layer

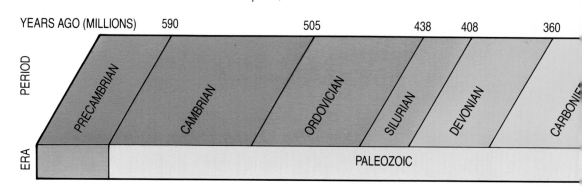

Eryops, a large amphibian ▶ *from the early Permian period. This hefty meat eater had a heavy skeleton, a massive, broad-mouthed skull, and sprawling legs. Amphibians usually lay their eggs in water, and reptiles, on land.*

Scientists believe the earth ▶ *to be about 4.5 billion years old, but the oldest recognizable large fossils are 600 million years old. Scientists have divided this fossil period into geological eras and periods, and these terms are used all over the world.*

YEARS AGO (MILLIONS)	590	505	438	408	360

PERIOD	PRECAMBRIAN	CAMBRIAN	ORDOVICIAN	SILURIAN	DEVONIAN	CARBONIF...

ERA	PALEOZOIC

upon layer, and in time turned into rock. Meanwhile, minerals filtered into the bones trapped within the sediment, and the bones turned to stone as well, becoming fossils. Over more millions of years, the old sea or lake bottom moved steadily up toward the surface, where, if we are lucky, we sometimes find fossilized dinosaur bones.

▲ *A scene in the great coal forests of Carboniferous times,* *before the dinosaurs appeared. The trees were huge.*

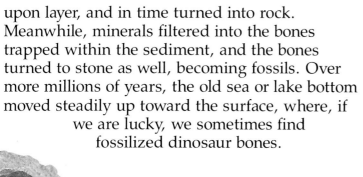

286	248	213	144	65	2

PERMIAN	TRIASSIC	JURASSIC	CRETACEOUS	TERTIARY	QUATERNARY
	MESOZOIC			CENOZOIC	

▲ *Skeleton of the small, lightly built sea reptile* Pachypleurosaurus, *from the middle Triassic period in Central Europe. This is a nothosaur, a long-necked reptile that swam by paddling and fed on fish. It lived at the same time as early dinosaurs but was not a dinosaur itself.*

2 The Triassic

The first dinosaurs lived in a warmer world than the one we live in today. As far as we know, there was no ice at the North Pole or the South Pole. This meant that temperatures around the globe were higher. Plants were different in many ways from the ones we know now. There were no grasses and no flowering plants of any kind. The only trees were conifers, like spruces, pines, cypresses, and monkey puzzles. There were also ferns.

EARLY EUROPEANS: The best-known early dinosaurs come from Europe and North America. In Germany, for example, some 220 million years ago, the scene was dominated by dinosaurs large and small. One was the 16-foot-long plant eater *Plateosaurus*. (Its Greek, scientific name means "flat reptile"; *saurus* in any word means "reptile.") It had a large, curved thumb claw that may have been used to rake leaves into its mouth.

The meat eaters of those early dinosaur days were small: *Procompsognathus* and *Halticosaurus* were about human height but much more lightly built. Clearly, they could not have fed on *Plateosaurus*, which was much too big. They must have preyed on the smaller animals that were around: frogs, turtles, lizardlike sphenodontids, and early mammals.

▲ *Reconstruction of* Plateosaurus, *the earliest large dinosaur. It fed on plants and used the large thumb claw to drag in food, which it cut up with sharp little teeth in its long jaws.*

◀ *These footprints, scientists tell us, belonged to a four-footed, meat-eating animal that was not a dinosaur. It lived during the Triassic period, in what is now central Europe.*

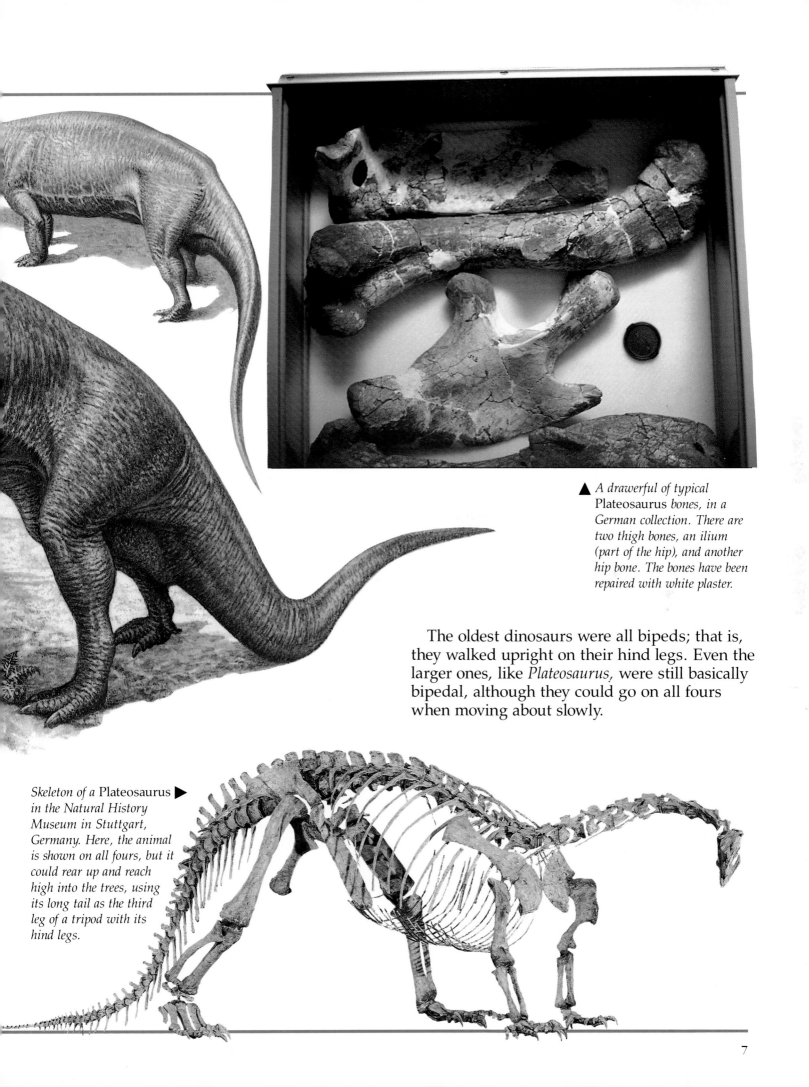

▲ *A drawerful of typical* Plateosaurus *bones, in a German collection. There are two thigh bones, an ilium (part of the hip), and another hip bone. The bones have been repaired with white plaster.*

The oldest dinosaurs were all bipeds; that is, they walked upright on their hind legs. Even the larger ones, like *Plateosaurus*, were still basically bipedal, although they could go on all fours when moving about slowly.

Skeleton of a Plateosaurus ▶ *in the Natural History Museum in Stuttgart, Germany. Here, the animal is shown on all fours, but it could rear up and reach high into the trees, using its long tail as the third leg of a tripod with its hind legs.*

Our First Dinosaurs

A t about the time *Plateosaurus* and *Halticosaurus* were roaming in Germany, or perhaps a little earlier, a meat eater named *Coelophysis* ("hollow form") was widespread in North America. Its remains have been found in New Mexico, Arizona, and possibly also in Connecticut. The first remains of this lightweight dinosaur were uncovered in 1881. There were only a few bones—pieces from a backbone, some rib fragments, hip bones, and limb bones. But a famous fossil hunter named Edward Cope identified three different species of *Coelophysis* from the bones.

THE MYSTERY SOLVED: In 1947, a group of scientists from the American Museum of Natural History in New York went back to the Ghost Ranch in northern New Mexico, where the bones had first been found. Now the collectors found many *Coelophysis* bones, all in a single level of rock formation, meaning that the dinosaurs had all died at about the same time. As the tons of rock and earth were removed over the next year, dozens of complete skeletons of *Coelophysis* were exposed. The skeletons lay over one another in a tangled mass. The scientists determined that a herd of these animals had been caught in a flash flood produced by a sudden downpour, and that their bodies had been washed along in the river and dumped on a sandbar. There

▲ *Edward Drinker Cope (1840–97) named* Coelophysis, *among many other dinosaur species.*

were small and large animals present. It became clear that the three species Cope had named were really just males, females, and the young of *one* species.

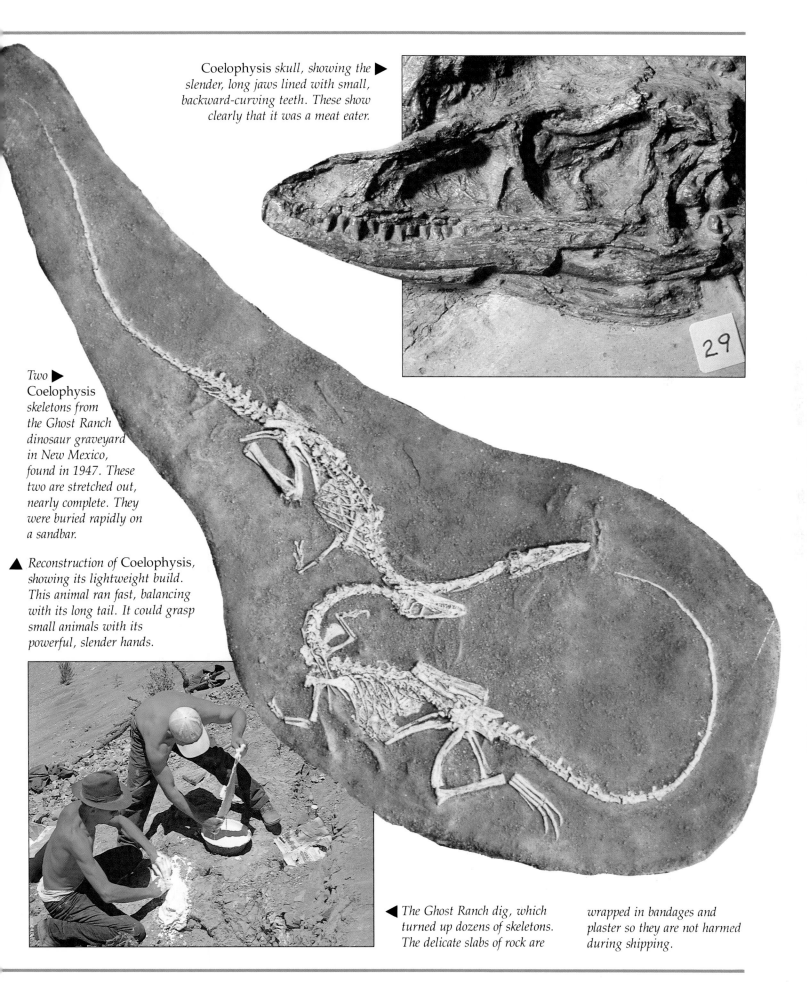

Coelophysis *skull, showing the* ▶ *slender, long jaws lined with small, backward-curving teeth. These show clearly that it was a meat eater.*

29

Two ▶
Coelophysis
skeletons from the Ghost Ranch dinosaur graveyard in New Mexico, found in 1947. These two are stretched out, nearly complete. They were buried rapidly on a sandbar.

▲ *Reconstruction of* Coelophysis, *showing its lightweight build. This animal ran fast, balancing with its long tail. It could grasp small animals with its powerful, slender hands.*

◀ *The Ghost Ranch dig, which turned up dozens of skeletons. The delicate slabs of rock are* *wrapped in bandages and plaster so they are not harmed during shipping.*

Who's Who

Dinosaurs belonged to a larger group of animals called archosaurs, which means "ruling reptiles." All of the archosaurs were descended from a group of Triassic reptiles called thecodonts.

FAMILY TREE: The archosaurs were made up of four groups. One, the crocodiles, is the only group still in existence. Another was the pterosaurs, which were flying reptiles. The other two groups were the reptiles we know as the dinosaurs. Each of these two groups of dinosaurs takes its name from the way its hip bones were formed. The saurischians, which means "lizard-hipped," were the meat eaters and also the large, long-necked plant eaters. The ornithischians, or "bird-hipped" dinosaurs, were all the others.

The first saurischians were meat eaters and stood on their hind legs. This left their front limbs free to hold onto their prey. Later, the plant-

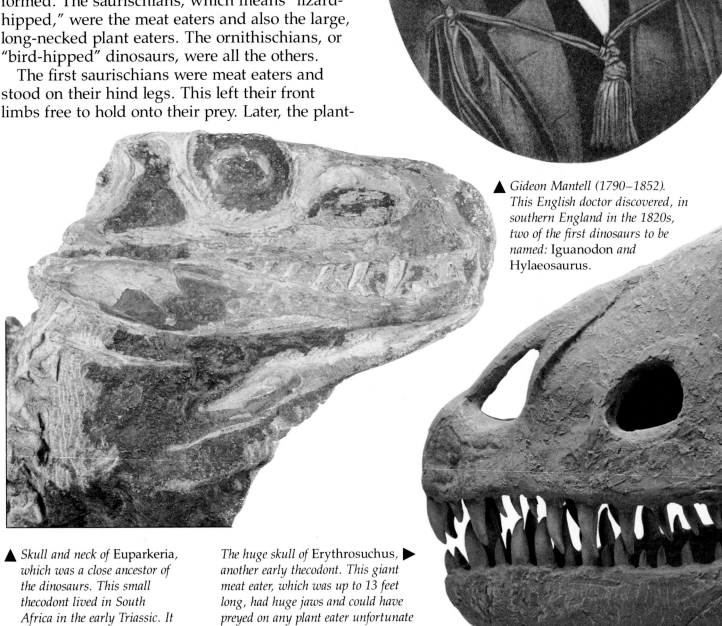

▲ Gideon Mantell (1790–1852). This English doctor discovered, in southern England in the 1820s, two of the first dinosaurs to be named: Iguanodon and Hylaeosaurus.

▲ Skull and neck of Euparkeria, which was a close ancestor of the dinosaurs. This small thecodont lived in South Africa in the early Triassic. It was a meat eater.

The huge skull of Erythrosuchus, ▶ another early thecodont. This giant meat eater, which was up to 13 feet long, had huge jaws and could have preyed on any plant eater unfortunate enough to cross its path.

10

eating saurischians evolved. But animals that eat plants need to have much longer intestines to digest vegetation. As their bellies got bigger and heavier, the largest plant eaters had to begin going on all fours.

NEW YEAR'S EVE: The dinosaurs were not the oldest animals on the earth. In fact, compared with the overall history of the planet, they appeared quite late. For most of the early history of the earth, no life at all existed. Then, for a very long time, there were only simple life-forms in the sea. The earth is 4,600 million years old, and the dinosaurs arose 230 million years ago. Here is one way to look at it: If the entire history of the earth were compressed into a single year, then the animals moved from the sea onto the land in about November. Dinosaurs appeared on December 12, and humans, only on the evening of December 31.

The dinosaurs are an order of fossil reptiles, and they are divided into two suborders, the Saurischia and Ornithischia. Each of these suborders falls into several families of related animals, the Plateosauridae, Coelophysidae, Diplodocidae, and so on. These terms refer to particular ranks in the great scheme of classification of all living (and extinct) plants and animals.

The lowest rank is usually the *species*, such as *Tyrannosaurus rex* or (in the case of man) *Homo sapiens*. Next up is the *genus* (plural, genera), such as *Tyrannosaurus* or *Homo*. Each genus may contain more than one species. The species and genera fall into families; modern examples are the Canidae (dogs, wolves, foxes), and the Equidae (horses, zebras, asses, and so on). The families are then grouped in suborders and orders, and the orders into classes, phyla, and kingdoms. An outline of the position, and main divisions, of the dinosaurs is:

Kingdom Animalia (all animals)
  Phylum Chordata (all animals with backbones)
    Class Reptilia (turtles, lizards, snakes, crocodiles, etc.)
      Order Dinosauria
        Suborder Saurischia
          Infraorder Sauropodomorpha
            Family Thecodontosauridae
            Family Plateosauridae
            Family Cetiosauridae
            Family Camarasauridae
            Family Diplodocidae
            Family Brachiosauridae
            Family Titanosauridae
          Infraorder Theropoda
            Family Coelophysidae
            Family Megalosauridae
            Family Tyrannosauridae
            Family Coeluridae
            Family Ornithomimidae
            Family Oviraptoridae
            Family Deinonychidae
          Infraorder Segnosauria (?)
        Suborder Ornithischia
          Infraorder Thyreophora
            Family Scelidosauridae
            Family Nodosauridae
            Family Ankylosauridae
            Family Stegosauridae
          Infraorder Ornithopoda
            Family Fabrosauridae
            Family Heterodontosauridae
            Family Hypsilophodontidae
            Family Iguanodontidae
            Family Hadrosauridae
         Infraorder Marginocephalia
            Family Pachycephalosauridae
            Family Ceratopsidae

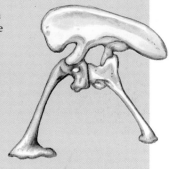

▲ *The three-pronged "lizard hip" of the meat-eating and giant plant-eating saurischians*

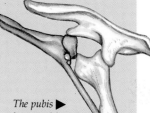

The pubis ▶ *bone (in blue) has swung back to form the "bird hip" of the plant-eating ornithischian dinosaurs.*

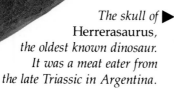

The skull of ▶ Herrerasaurus, *the oldest known dinosaur. It was a meat eater from the late Triassic in Argentina.*

▲ The pelvis of a large prosauropod being excavated in Lesotho, in southern Africa. The hammer gives an idea of scale.

◄ The hind limb of Massospondylus being dug out in southern Africa. The bones are exposed this way during excavation and are then packed for transport to the museum.

During late Triassic and early Jurassic times, about 225 million to 187 million years ago, a group of dinosaurs called prosauropods ("before lizard-feet") flourished briefly. *Plateosaurus* (see pages 6–7 and 16–17) was one of them. The prosauropods looked about halfway between the two-footed, meat-eating theropods ("mammal-feet") and the huge four-footed, plant-eating sauropods ("lizard-feet").

FALLING IN: One of the first dinosaurs to be discovered was a small prosauropod called *Thecodontosaurus*, found in southern England in the 1830s. All the *Thecodontosaurus* bones have been found in ancient fissures, or open cave systems, formed during the Triassic. Small animals apparently fell down these fissures and became trapped. Scientists can now excavate these fissures. (Excavating means digging to find things that have been buried over time.) The fissures provide rare information about the smaller, more delicate dinosaurs.

OTHER PROSAUROPODS: The remains of *Massospondylus* ("massive vertebrae"; vertebrae are the bones in the spine) have been found on five continents. It was lightly built and reached about 20 feet in length. Although it could walk on two or four feet, it seems to have preferred to walk on four. Later prosauropods, such as *Riojasaurus*, grew to almost twice that size. By early Jurassic times, many forms, such as *Vulcanodon*, were on the borderline of becoming true sauropods, the giants of the Jurassic and Cretaceous (see pages 24–29).

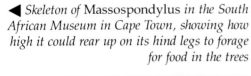

◄ *Skeleton of* Massospondylus *in the South African Museum in Cape Town, showing how high it could rear up on its hind legs to forage for food in the trees*

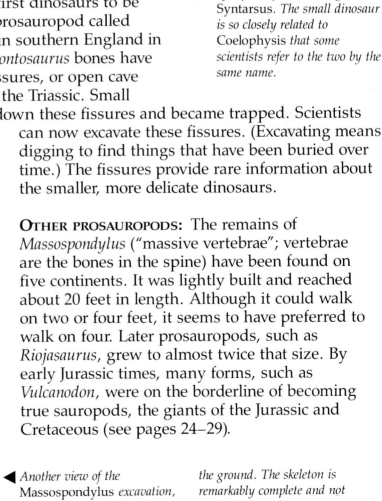

▲ Massospondylus *is attacked by a pack of meat-eating* Syntarsus. *The small dinosaur is so closely related to* Coelophysis *that some scientists refer to the two by the same name.*

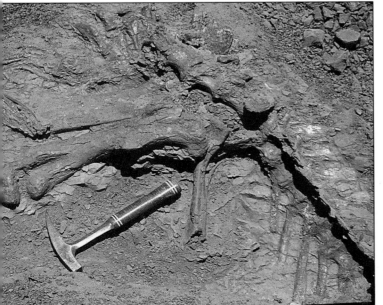

◄ *Another view of the* Massospondylus *excavation, showing parts of the backbone and hind limb as they lay in the ground. The skeleton is remarkably complete and not much damaged by water movement over time.*

Deep Time and Moving Continents

Geologists are scientists who study the history of the earth by looking at its changing rock forms. They deal in almost unimaginably long spans of time. The evidence for geological ages has to be obtained from the rocks and fossils that are found in layer upon layer (the layers are called strata) that are exposed to view. In the early 19th century, geologists noticed that the deepest rocks (the oldest ones) contained the fossils of very simple plants and animals. Higher up, fishes and land plants were found, then amphibians, then reptiles, then mammals and birds. These early geologists also realized that there were particular groups of fossils that were always found together and that seemed to be often found in particular rock formations. These two ideas—progress in the history of life, and fossils being found together in certain kinds of rock—allowed the early geologists to figure out which rocks were the oldest, and to identify rocks of similar age by the fossils they contained, even if they were found in different parts of the world.

FINDING THE DATES: Having gotten the rocks roughly into order, geologists began to work on ways of finding the exact dates of the rocks in millions of years. This is done by looking at rates of change, or decay, in the natural radioactivity present in rocks. The older the rock, the more decay will have taken place.

HOLD STILL! Though it seems bizarre, the surface of the earth is actually made up of many large, rocky plates that are in constant motion. The movement can be measured and is felt in the form of earthquakes. During Triassic times, all the continents were fused together as one, and dinosaurs could roam freely all over the world. For example, the North American prosauropod *Anchisaurus* has also been found in South Africa. After the Triassic, however, new seaways formed, the Atlantic and Indian oceans opened up, and the continents moved slowly but surely toward the positions they are in now.

▲ *The dinosaur-bearing rocks in the badlands of Alberta, Canada, show the layering of the rocks.*

▲ Excavation of a duck-billed dinosaur, showing the backbone in the middle, ribs above, and tail below

▼ The badlands of the South Saskatchewan River in Alberta, Canada. Sudden rains wash away layers of soft sediments, leaving the ancient, layered rocks bare of plant life. These are "good lands" for dinosaur hunting.

The changing face of the earth ▶ over the last 200 million years. When the dinosaurs arose in the Triassic, all the continents were fused to form a single great landmass. The North Atlantic opened up in the Jurassic, and the South Atlantic, in the Cretaceous. Southern continents were also on the move, and by 100 million years ago, the layout of the world was more like it is today.

200 million years ago

100 million years ago

present day

Herds of Dinosaurs

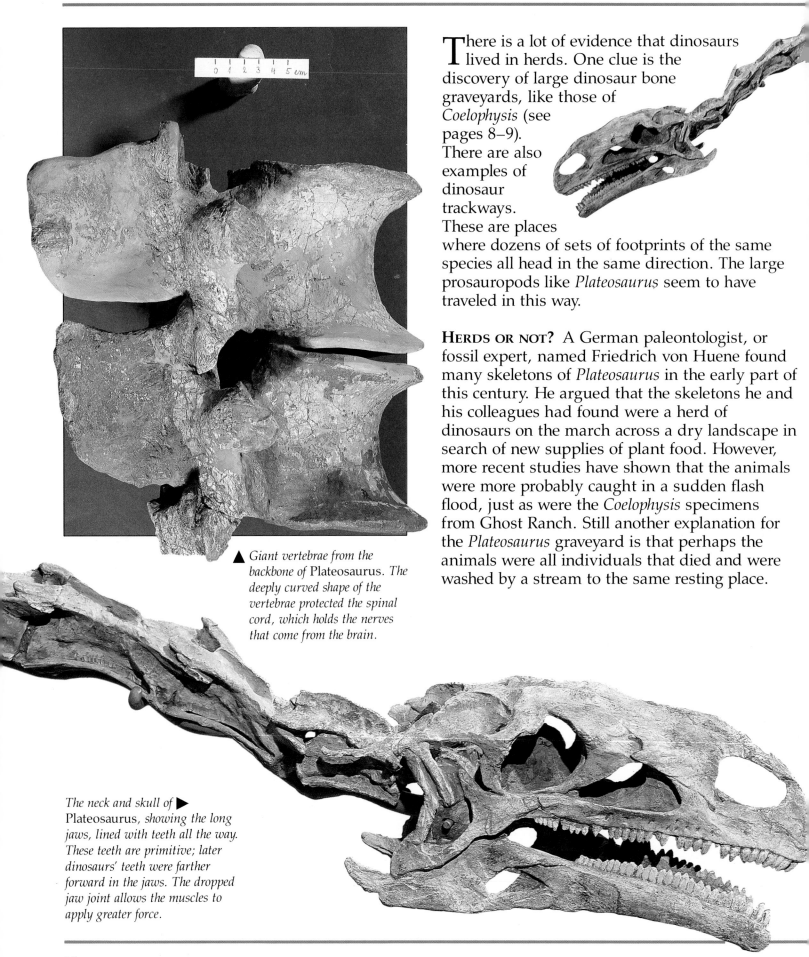

There is a lot of evidence that dinosaurs lived in herds. One clue is the discovery of large dinosaur bone graveyards, like those of *Coelophysis* (see pages 8–9). There are also examples of dinosaur trackways. These are places where dozens of sets of footprints of the same species all head in the same direction. The large prosauropods like *Plateosaurus* seem to have traveled in this way.

HERDS OR NOT? A German paleontologist, or fossil expert, named Friedrich von Huene found many skeletons of *Plateosaurus* in the early part of this century. He argued that the skeletons he and his colleagues had found were a herd of dinosaurs on the march across a dry landscape in search of new supplies of plant food. However, more recent studies have shown that the animals were more probably caught in a sudden flash flood, just as were the *Coelophysis* specimens from Ghost Ranch. Still another explanation for the *Plateosaurus* graveyard is that perhaps the animals were all individuals that died and were washed by a stream to the same resting place.

▲ *Giant vertebrae from the backbone of* Plateosaurus. *The deeply curved shape of the vertebrae protected the spinal cord, which holds the nerves that come from the brain.*

The neck and skull of ▶ Plateosaurus, *showing the long jaws, lined with teeth all the way. These teeth are primitive; later dinosaurs' teeth were farther forward in the jaws. The dropped jaw joint allows the muscles to apply greater force.*

◀ Skeleton of Plateosaurus, in the Stuttgart Natural History Museum in Germany. The long, snakelike neck allowed the animal to reach high into food-bearing trees. Vast herds of these animals have been found in the sandstone of Germany and France.

Friedrich von Huene ▶ (1875–1970), the great early expert on Plateosaurus

▼ Excavation of the Ghost Ranch Coelophysis skeletons. Like many finds of Plateosaurus, these had been preserved after a flash flood.

3 The Jurassic

In the Jurassic period, climates were still warm, as in the Triassic, but they were probably not as dry. The landscape was covered with tall conifer trees and many low-growing plants at the sides of broad, meandering rivers. The winters were cooler but had no snow.

The early Jurassic dinosaurs were mainly like those of the late Triassic. There were prosauropods and there were meat eaters like *Coelophysis*, with a few new plant-eating types (see pages 20–21). During the middle and late Jurassic, some major new groups came onto the scene. These included large meat eaters (see pages 22–23), the giant plant-eating sauropods (see pages 24–27), the stegosaurs (see pages 28–29), the bipedal, or two-legged, plant eaters (see pages 30–31), and new small meat eaters (see pages 32–33).

DINOSAUR RACE: The late Jurassic rocks in parts of Utah and Colorado contain some of the best-known dinosaurs: *Allosaurus, Apatosaurus* (which used to be called *Brontosaurus*), *Diplodocus, Stegosaurus*, and others. These were all first collected in the early days of American paleontology, between 1870 and 1900. The work was done by teams sent out by the arch-rivals Edward Cope and Othniel Marsh. The collectors

▲ *Othniel Charles Marsh (1831–99), the great dinosaur hunter and rival of Edward Cope*

The meat eater Allosaurus ▶ *stalks its prey, while carcasses and skeletons lying on the riverbank are on their way to becoming fossils.*

dug out the huge bones at great speed and often in awful conditions, and sent them East by the trainload. Between them, Cope and Marsh named 130 new species of dinosaurs from this part of America.

This crew of dinosaur hunters, ▶ *led by Othniel Marsh (center back) operated in the Western Territories in 1872. Guns and knives were part of their gear.*

◀ *Dinosaur bones being carefully picked out of the rock at Dinosaur National Monument, in Colorado. Here, during the Jurassic, hundreds of skeletons were washed together and dumped on a sandbar.*

▲ Vast thicknesses of
Jurassic sediments,
containing dinosaur
bones, are exposed in the
area of Dinosaur
National Monument, in
Utah and in Colorado.

The First Armored Dinosaurs

Three different armored dinosaurs first appeared in the early Jurassic—one in southern England, one in the southwestern United States, and one in southern Africa. All were "bird-hipped" dinosaurs. In England, *Scelidosaurus* ("limb reptile") was named in 1860 from some odd bones and a nearly complete skeleton. Recently, some new *Scelidosaurus* bones have been found, and scientists have had a chance to gather more information about the animal. It was 13 feet long and probably walked most of the time on all fours. It was a plant eater, as shown by its teeth, and it had broad, hooflike toenails. Its armor consisted of many oval-shaped, bony plates, each two to four inches long, lying in long rows over the neck, the back, the sides, and the tail. These bony plates were attached firmly into the skin and probably protected the animal from attacks by meat eaters.

AMERICAN COUSIN: The early American armored dinosaur is *Scutellosaurus* ("reptile with small shields"). Just named in 1981, it was obviously a close relative of *Scelidosaurus*, though it was nearly twice as long. But the armor was much

▲ *Skeleton of* Heterodontosaurus, *from the early Jurassic of southern Africa. It had tusks, which were unusual in a plant-eating dinosaur.*

◄ *The Lesotho Red Beds, in Africa, have produced many of the best skeletons of early dinosaurs, especially* Heterodontosaurus. *Because many layers are exposed, dinosaur hunters can scour the ground for bones.*

Excavation of a small ► *dinosaur skeleton in the Lesotho Red Beds. Here, South African paleontologists A.W. Crompton and R.F. Ewer are at work.*

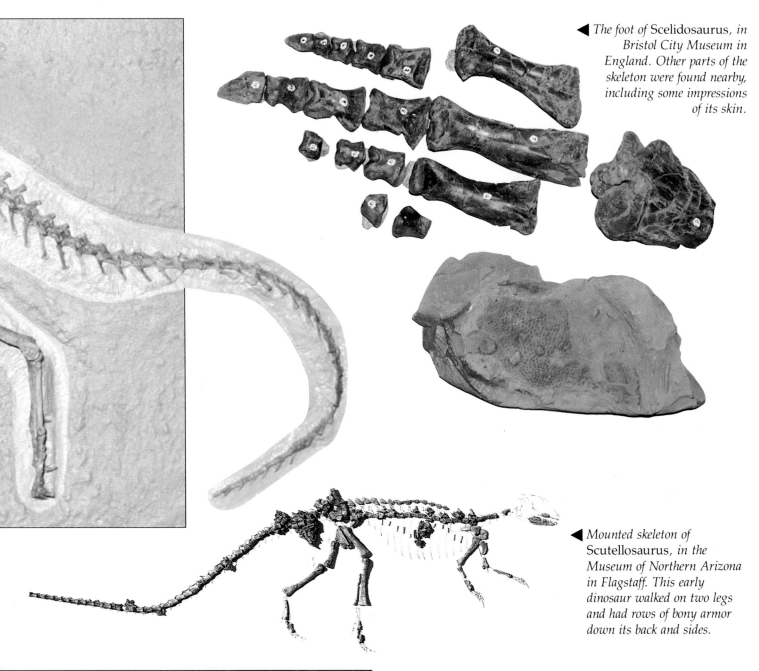

The foot of Scelidosaurus, in Bristol City Museum in England. Other parts of the skeleton were found nearby, including some impressions of its skin.

Mounted skeleton of Scutellosaurus, in the Museum of Northern Arizona in Flagstaff. This early dinosaur walked on two legs and had rows of bony armor down its back and sides.

like *Scelidosaurus*'s. It was probably an ancestor of the stegosaurs (see pages 28–29) and the ankylosaurs (see pages 54–55).

Heterodontosaurus ("reptile with different kinds of teeth"), the early African armored dinosaur, was somewhat different from the other two. It was a small plant eater, only four feet long. *Heterodontosaurus*, named in 1962, did not have any body armor, but it did have very unusual teeth. In particular, many specimens, perhaps males, had sharp, tusklike side teeth. These may have been used for defense, just the way pigs use their sharp fangs to defend themselves.

The Big Meat Eaters

For the first 40 million years of dinosaur evolution, there were no meat-eating dinosaurs large enough to eat other dinosaurs. But in the middle Jurassic, large meat-eating dinosaurs began appearing. One of the first of these new and fearsome predators was *Megalosaurus*.

WHAT IS IT? The first bone of *Megalosaurus* was actually found in 1677, but it was thought to be a bone from a giant human. At that time, of course, nobody knew anything of dinosaurs. Over the next years, more bones came to light in the limestone quarries north of Oxford, England. One of these was a jawbone that had large teeth with zigzag edges, like the edges of steak knives. An English professor of geology named William Buckland (1784–1856) realized that the bones all came from

The first dinosaur ever to be named—Megalosaurus, from the middle Jurassic of England. This animal may have been an ancestor of the later giant meat eaters.

▼ *Skull of the meat eater* Allosaurus, *showing the knifelike teeth. The skull had an extremely light but strong construction, using the minimum amount of bone. This made the head easy to support and move quickly.*

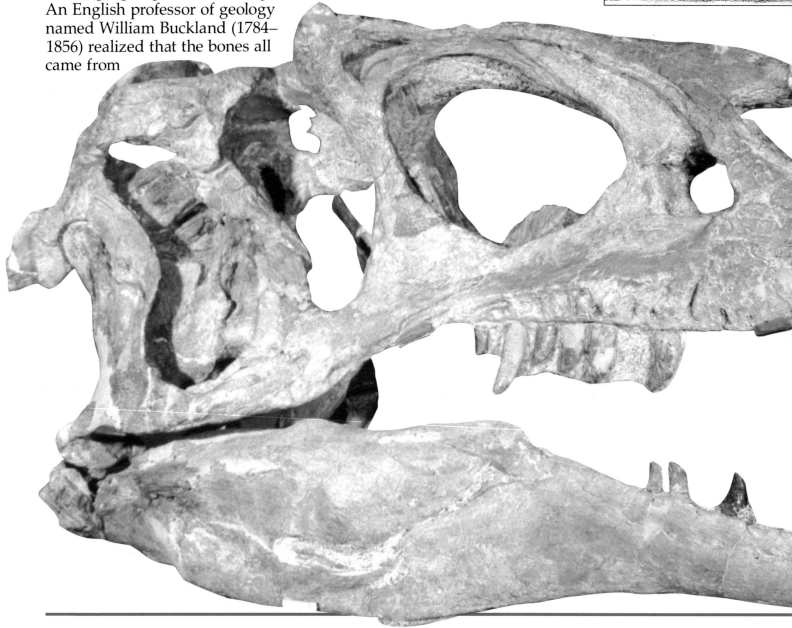

some kind of giant reptile. In 1824, he named it *Megalosaurus*—"big reptile" in Greek. This was the first dinosaur ever to be named.

EVEN BIGGER: In the late Jurassic, the meat eaters grew even larger, and there were more different kinds of them. In Utah and Colorado, for example, there were two well-known forms, *Ceratosaurus* ("horned reptile") and *Allosaurus* ("strange reptile"). *Ceratosaurus* was 13.5 feet long, and *Allosaurus* was three times that, 39 feet. Both would have been able to attack and eat many of the dinosaurs around at that time. Even the large sauropods (see pages 24–27) were not completely safe. *Allosaurus* was probably large enough and fast enough to attack at least the youngest, oldest, and weakest sauropods.

◀ *Model of* Allosaurus, *showing its running style. The long tail was held straight out behind as a balancing rod at high speeds.*

▼ *This very good specimen of the skull of* Allosaurus *is being prepared. It was preserved nearly uncrushed in the late Jurassic rocks of Colorado.*

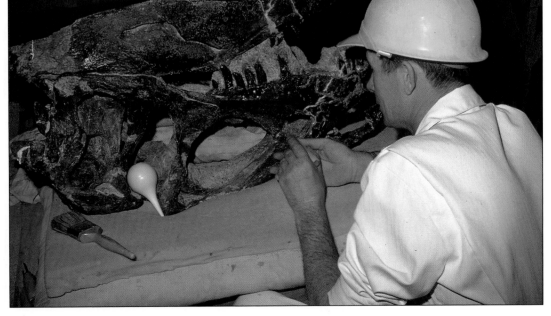

The Giant Plant Eaters

◀ Camarasaurus *browsing on vegetation in late Jurassic times. The long neck allowed the dinosaur to feed high in the trees.* Camarasaurus *had an unusually shaped boxlike skull and teeth like chisels.*

▼ *The short-snouted skull of* Camarasaurus *shows how few teeth it had, compared with its earlier relative,* Plateosaurus *(see page 16). The openings in the skull are for the nostrils, eye sockets, and jaw muscle attachments.*

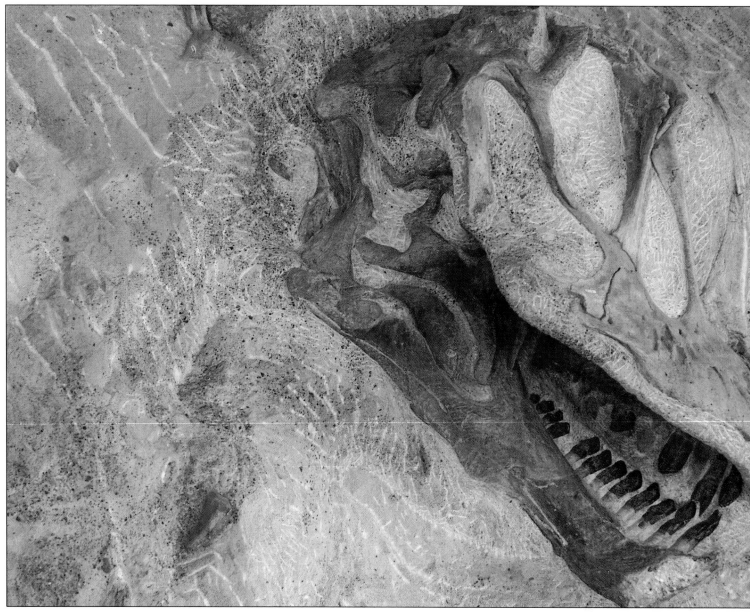

The giant plant-eating dinosaurs are known as sauropods. One of the first true sauropods was *Barapasaurus* ("big-legged lizard") from India, which is known from hundreds of bones found scattered over a wide area. The teeth of meat-eating dinosaurs were found among these large bones. One possible reason is that the *Barapasaurus* were feeding on the carcasses of the meat eaters.

NOT A WHALE: During the 1830s, several enormous vertebrae came to light in different parts of England. At first, these bones were thought to come from the backbones of whales. The English scientist Richard Owen (1804–92) thought the bones belonged to a giant sea crocodile, and so he named it *Cetiosaurus* ("whale reptile") in 1841. It was only in 1869, when much more of the skeleton was found, that it was identified as a dinosaur. These animals were important middle Jurassic sauropods and grew up to 59 feet long, as long as about five cars.

ROCK EATERS: The real flowering of the sauropods happened in the late Jurassic. One of the most common sauropods then was *Camarasaurus* ("chambered reptile"). It was found in the area called the Morrison Formation, on the eastern edge of the Rocky Mountains between New Mexico and Montana. Many other sauropod bones have been found there. *Camarasaurus* was about 59 feet long and heavily built. It seems to have swallowed stones to grind up food in its stomach, in the same way that chickens do.

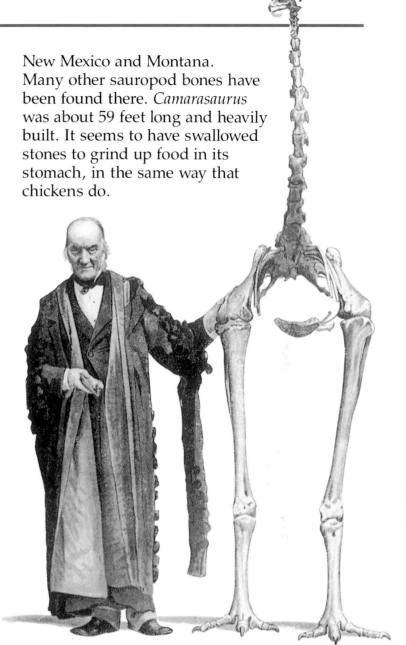

▲ *Richard Owen (1804–92), with a fossil bird called* Dinornis

▲ *Vertebrae of the early sauropod* Cetiosaurus *from the middle Jurassic of England. It was named by Richard Owen.*

Digging up the leg bone of an ▶ *early sauropod,* Barapasaurus, *from the early Jurassic of India.*

The Largest Plant Eaters

The best-known sauropods belong to two groups called the brachiosaurids and the diplodocids. *Brachiosaurus* ("reptile with arms"), one of the first group, was first reported in Colorado, where an incomplete skeleton was found. More information about this dinosaur soon came from Africa. In 1907, a German prospector chanced upon a rich dinosaur deposit in Tanzania. A series of massive expeditions was set up, and over 275 tons of fossil bones were carried to the coast and sent to Germany. One of the best specimens was a complete skeleton of *Brachiosaurus*.

A DIFFERENT WORLD: It may seem unusual that the same kind of dinosaur was found in North America and in Africa. However, remember that at this time, all the continents were joined together (see page 15), and the large sauropods could wander freely across the globe.

The total length of *Brachiosaurus* was 74.5 feet, and it could raise its head to the amazing height of 39 feet, the height of a four-story building. Like the other brachiosaurids, it had forelegs longer than its hind legs, so it was not able to rear up on its hind legs as the diplodocids were. But to compensate, it had a long, powerful, giraffelike neck.

THE BIG ONES: The diplodocids were more lightly built and equipped with long, whiplike tails. *Diplodocus* ("double-beamed animal") grew to 88.5 feet, and *Apatosaurus* reached 69 feet. They had long skulls and peglike teeth. Since 1970,

some even larger sauropods have been reported from North America: *Supersaurus*, perhaps 82 to 98 feet long; *Ultrasaurus*, perhaps 98 feet; and the incredible *Seismosaurus* ("reptile that shakes the earth"), which might have been as much as 131 feet, about four buses long. If this estimate is correct, it is the longest living thing ever to have been discovered.

▲ *The front of the jaws of* Diplodocus, *showing the many peglike teeth crowded closely together and rooted deeply in the jawbones. These teeth were used for tearing up large quantities of food for swallowing.*

▲ Diplodocus's *"chevron" bone, the reason for its name, "double-beamed animal." Two* chevron bones lay below the tail vertebrae and protected the tail as it dragged along the ground.

◄ *Skeleton of the longest complete dinosaur known,* Diplodocus carnegii, *named for Andrew Carnegie, the wealthy American who paid for the expedition. Compare its length to that of the plant eater* Iguanodon *to its right.*

Reconstruction of the largest ► *discovered dinosaurs.* Brachiosaurus (middle) *is known from nearly complete skeletons from Tanzania and from the western United States. The other two,* Ultrasaurus (left) *and* Supersaurus (right), *are based on partial skeletons. We know that they were very, very large, but their exact sizes are hard to estimate.*

The Plated Dinosaurs

In the middle and late Jurassic, a remarkable new group of dinosaurs appeared: the stegosaurs. These animals had rows of bony plates or spikes on their backs and tails. The *Stegosaurus* ("roof reptile") had leaf-shaped plates sticking up from its back. There is some disagreement about whether the plates marched down the back in even pairs or alternated in an overlapping pattern. A slow-moving plant eater, it was the largest of the stegosaurs, reaching about 25 feet in length. In addition to the plates, it had sharp spikes, or spines, on its tail, which must surely have been lethal if the tail was whipped around.

A MYSTERY: It has usually been assumed that the plates and spikes protected the stegosaurs from attack by large meat eaters. This may have been partly true, but the plates did not actually cover the vulnerable sides of the body. It may be that they also were used for temperature control. In life, the plates were covered with skin, which contained many blood vessels. In hot weather, blood would be pumped to the plates, and heat would be given off into the air, cooling the animals. On colder days, the blood vessels to the plates may have shut down, saving body heat.

SMALL AND SPIKY: In Tanzania in Africa lived a much smaller but much pricklier stegosaur called *Kentrosaurus* ("pointed reptile"). It was only 8.2 feet long. It had a fearsome-looking procession of spikes going down its back in pairs, and a long spike jutting out of each hip joint.

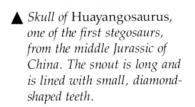

▲ *Skull of Huayangosaurus, one of the first stegosaurs, from the middle Jurassic of China. The snout is long and is lined with small, diamond-shaped teeth.*

▼ *Reconstruction of the late Jurassic stegosaur* Kentrosaurus. *Its hip bones show that it was, like all stegosaurs, an ornithischian, or "bird-hipped," dinosaur.*

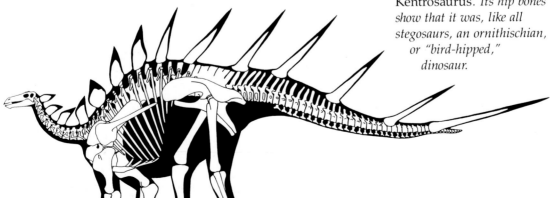

Excavation of the tiny bones of a young Stegosaurus *found in late Jurassic sediments at Dinosaur National Monument in Colorado in the 1970s. It was probably only a year old when it died.*

A stegosaur gallery: ▶
Stegosaurus *(top left),*
Tuojiangosaurus *(top right),*
Kentrosaurus *(bottom right),*
Lexovisaurus *(middle), and*
Dacentrurus *(bottom left).*

▼ *The best-known stegosaur,* Stegosaurus, *as a mounted skeleton and as a model. The* Stegosaurus *is the state fossil of Colorado.*

Stegosaurus

Stegosaurus had a narrow body and a heavy, spiked tail. Its back legs were almost twice as long as its front legs. This plant-eater may have reared on its hind legs to reach tall vegetation.

Stegosaurus armatus

The New Plant Eaters

Other new groups of plant eaters developed in the late Jurassic. Earlier, in the late Triassic or early Jurassic, ornithopods had arisen. These were two-legged ornithischian dinosaurs with no armor. Now, new forms were taking shape.

FAST RUNNER: *Dryosaurus* ("wood reptile"), from North America and Tanzania in Africa, was 10 to 13 feet long. It was an agile and active biped. Its head was short, and its teeth were highly specialized for chopping up tough plants. The sauropods of the same period had peglike teeth that could only really have dealt with soft leaves, and it may be that the ornithopods outlasted them because of their more advanced eating equipment. *Dryosaurus* had short arms and long legs for rapid running. *Dryosaurus* seems to have lived all over the world.

Camptosaurus ("flexible reptile") was a close relative. It was a 16- to 23-foot-long ornithopod, known in North America and Europe.

The skull of *Camptosaurus* is long and almost horselike in shape. The tips of the snout and lower jaw have no teeth at all, only a sharp beak made of bone. Behind this lies a series of broad teeth that could perform a primitive kind of chewing action.

▼ *View of the inside of the right upper jaw of* Camptosaurus. *The ridges on the teeth made a grinding surface for dealing with tough plants.*

Using skeletons from the ▶ *late Jurassic of North America, scientists have reconstructed a scene of the large meat eater* Allosaurus *attacking the plant-eating* Camptosaurus.

◀ *Vertebrae of* **Camptosaurus,** *a large dinosaur from the late Jurassic. The smallest bones come from the end of the tail, and the larger ones from the back.*

Skull of **Dryosaurus altus** ▲ *from North America, which had a very close relative in Africa. Plants were broken up with the broad cheek teeth in the middle and back parts of the jaws.*

The skeleton of **Camptosaurus** ▼ *from the late Jurassic of North America. This large ornithopod walked either on all fours or on its hind limbs alone, especially when it was running fast.*

▲ *Skull of* **Dryosaurus,** *showing the powerful teeth and the shortened face. The skull was in many ways the same shape as a sheep's.*

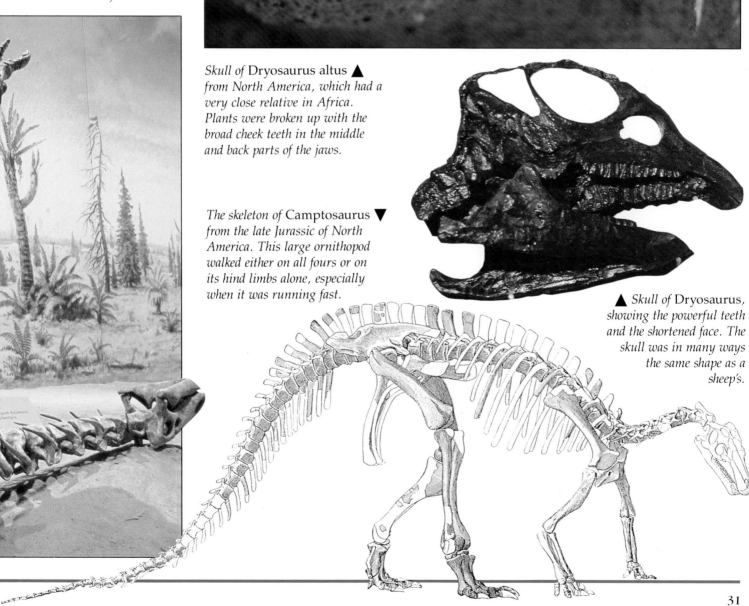

Small Meat Eaters and Birds

In Solnhofen, Germany, the sediments of an ancient body of water called a lagoon have preserved some amazing fossils of small dinosaurs and other animals. The detail is so fantastic that not only are tiny bones seen complete in every detail, but also the soft body outlines of fishes and lizards. One can even find completely soft-bodied animals like worms and jellyfishes. The sedimentary deposits of this lagoon have turned into a very fine limestone that is still mined for fossils.

PRETTY JAW: In the late 1850s, a remarkable little skeleton was found at Solnhofen. This was a three-foot-long, bipedal, meat-eating dinosaur named *Compsognathus* ("pretty jaw"). Its head was lightweight, had very large eye sockets, and rows of tiny, needle-sharp teeth. The legs were thin and the tail was extremely long. Inside the rib cage was the skeleton of a large lizard, the last meal of this small dinosaur.

FIRST BIRD: Another small, lightweight skeleton was found at Solnhofen in 1861. The bones were almost exactly like those of *Compsognathus* and

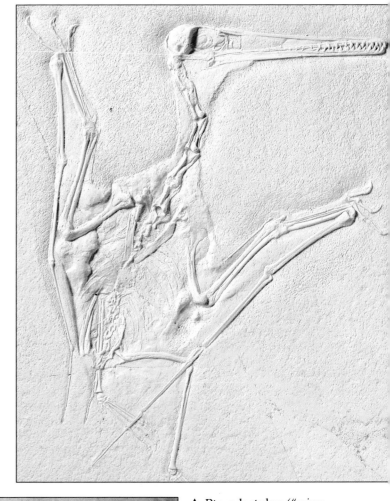

▲ Pterodactylus *("wing finger"), a pigeon-size flying pterosaur, beautifully preserved in the mudstones of Solnhofen. Traces of the skin around its throat and wings can even be seen.*

◄ *Skeleton of* Compsognathus. *This is the smallest known adult dinosaur. Inside the rib cage are the remains of its last meal, a fast-moving lizard called* Bavarisaurus. *This meant* Compsognathus *had to be extremely fast to catch it.*

The rarest fossil of all, a ▶ *complete specimen of* Archaeopteryx. *The body is stretched out, with the head bent back because of the drying out of the body. The wing and tail feathers are clear. This bird was still very much like a reptile.*

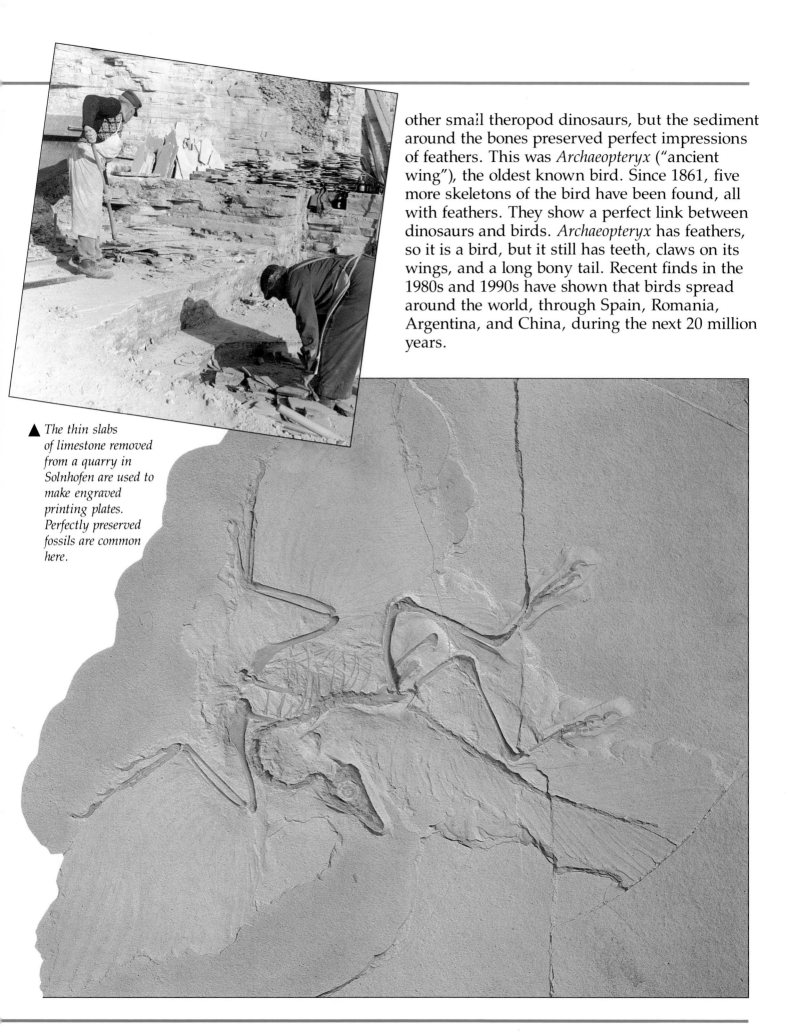

other small theropod dinosaurs, but the sediment around the bones preserved perfect impressions of feathers. This was *Archaeopteryx* ("ancient wing"), the oldest known bird. Since 1861, five more skeletons of the bird have been found, all with feathers. They show a perfect link between dinosaurs and birds. *Archaeopteryx* has feathers, so it is a bird, but it still has teeth, claws on its wings, and a long bony tail. Recent finds in the 1980s and 1990s have shown that birds spread around the world, through Spain, Romania, Argentina, and China, during the next 20 million years.

▲ *The thin slabs of limestone removed from a quarry in Solnhofen are used to make engraved printing plates. Perfectly preserved fossils are common here.*

The Early Cretaceous World

During the early Cretaceous, from 144 million to 98 million years ago, the continents were just beginning to show signs of breaking up, and different dinosaurs were appearing in different parts of the world. Climates were still warm and mild. Many of the dinosaur fossils have been found close to rivers, and many other fossils have been found alongside them: frogs, salamanders, turtles, crocodilians, lizards, the earliest snakes, flying pterosaurs (often quite large ones), and early birds and mammals.

NEWCOMERS: During this period, dinosaurs evolved into several new groups. There were new forms of plant eaters with highly efficient jaws, and they probably browsed on low bushes and trees in huge herds. There were new kinds of armored plant-eating dinosaurs, and these were preyed upon by new meat eaters, many of them armed with vicious, slashing claws. The giant sauropods were still around, but by now very rare; this was a big change from the late Jurassic world.

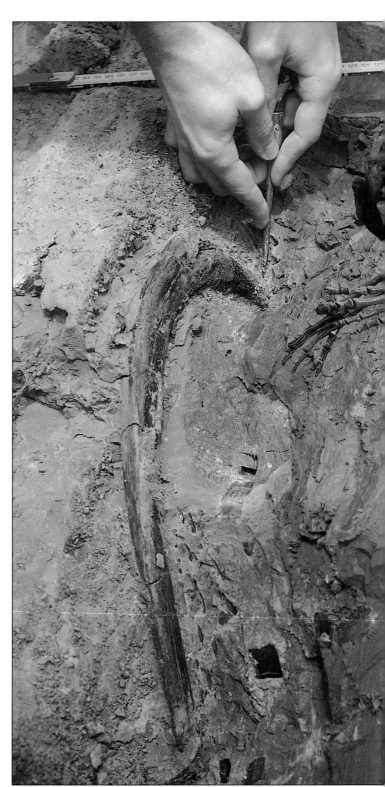

▼ Another excavation in the Isle of Wight. Many, many dinosaur skeletons come to light every year, after storms wash off soft sediments along the coast.

▲ Skeleton of Iguanodon being excavated in the Isle of Wight, southern England. This is part of the area called the Weald.

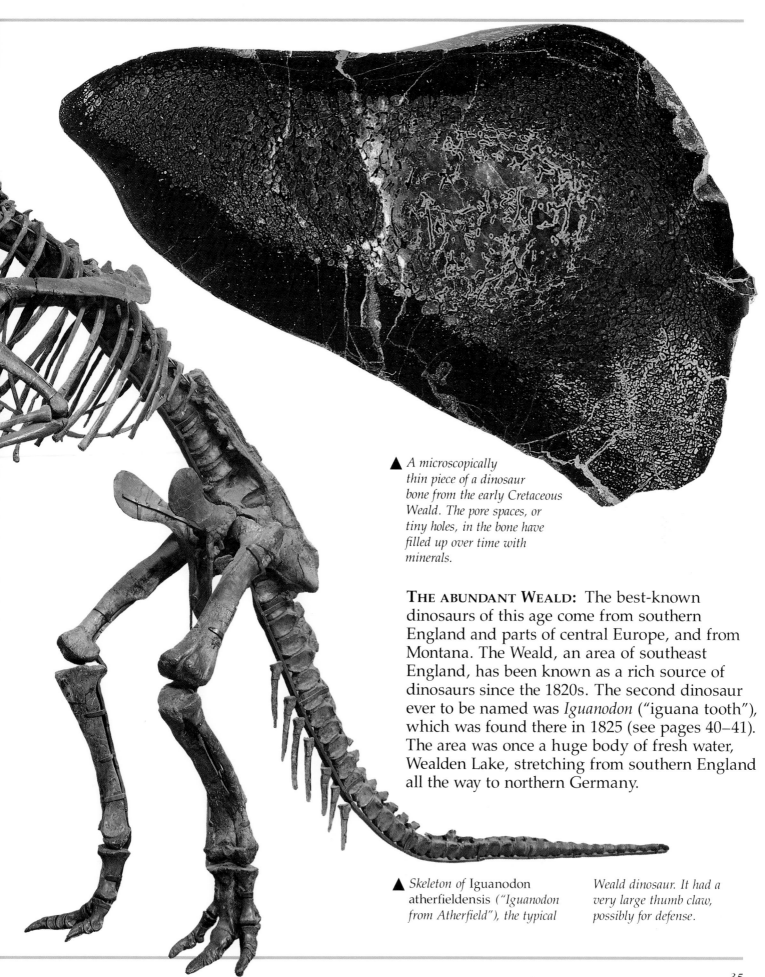

▲ A microscopically
thin piece of a dinosaur
bone from the early Cretaceous
Weald. The pore spaces, or
tiny holes, in the bone have
filled up over time with
minerals.

THE ABUNDANT WEALD: The best-known
dinosaurs of this age come from southern
England and parts of central Europe, and from
Montana. The Weald, an area of southeast
England, has been known as a rich source of
dinosaurs since the 1820s. The second dinosaur
ever to be named was *Iguanodon* ("iguana tooth"),
which was found there in 1825 (see pages 40–41).
The area was once a huge body of fresh water,
Wealden Lake, stretching from southern England
all the way to northern Germany.

▲ *Skeleton of* Iguanodon
atherfieldensis *("Iguanodon
from Atherfield"), the typical*
*Weald dinosaur. It had a
very large thumb claw,
possibly for defense.*

The Heyday of the Ornithopods

The first really successful ornithischians (or bird-hipped dinosaurs) were the hypsilophodontids ("high-ridged teeth"). They first arose in the late Jurassic, with forms like *Dryosaurus* spreading out into the world. In the early Cretaceous, the hypsilophodontids traveled even more widely. They have been found in North America, Europe, South America, Australia, and even Antarctica.

NOT BABIES: The best-known dinosaur of this group is *Hypsilophodon* itself, from the Weald deposits in England. The first skeletons were found in 1849 but were thought to be *Iguanodon* babies. Only later, when more complete skeletons were found, was the confusion cleared up. Many skeletons are still turning up today.

CHEWING CHAMPS: *Hypsilophodon* was one of the smallest and fastest plant-eating dinosaurs of its time. It had a short skull, no teeth at the front of its jaws (this "beak" was typical of the ornithischians), and a long row of cheek teeth farther back. Like a sheep, *Hypsilophodon* must have nipped off leaves with the toothless front part of its snout, moved them back with its tongue, and "chewed" them in a way that only ornithopods did. *Hypsilophodon, Iguanodon,* and their relatives could flex their cheeks in and out. There was an extra joint between the bones along the side of the face, and as the jaws closed around a mouthful of leaves, the upper jaw splayed outward. When the lower jaw moved down, the upper jaw moved back inward. This remarkable in-and-out chewing technique may have given these advanced ornithopods the edge over other plant-eating dinosaurs that could not chew their food. Like all other reptiles, most dinosaurs could simply open and shut their mouths like the hinge of a door, and food had to be swallowed unchewed.

Excavation of a ▶ Hypsilophodon *skeleton. This small dinosaur, about seven feet long, was extremely common. It probably traveled in large herds, browsing on low bushes.*

Reconstruction of ▶ Hypsilophodon foxi *("Fox's Hypsilophodon") based on several skeletons. At first, it was thought to have perched in trees. But the strong feet could not grasp branches and are clearly designed for fast running.*

▼ *Skull of one of the last hypsilophodontids,* Parksosaurus, *from Alberta, Canada. The short jaws have ridged teeth in the cheek region, which were used for cutting up plant food. There were no teeth at the front, only a bony plate.*

▲ *One level of rocks in the Weald of the Isle of Wight in southern England is called the* Hypsilophodon *Bed, because so many of these dinosaurs have been found there.*

◀ Thescelosaurus, *a later relative of* Hypsilophodon. *Its backward-pointing pubic bone at the hip shows that it is ornithischian, or "bird-hipped." (Compare it to* Plateosaurus *on page 17, a "lizard-hipped" saurischian.)*

The Sickle Claws

People often mistakenly think that all the most exciting dinosaurs were found years ago. In North America and Europe especially, where fossils have been collected for years, how could there possibly be anything new?

NEW ARRIVALS: Dramatic discoveries in recent years, however, have proved this idea wrong. Two dinosaurs unearthed only recently— *Deinonychus* ("terrible claw") from Montana and *Baryonyx* ("heavy claw") from Surrey, England— have proved that spectacular new kinds of meat-eating dinosaurs came into being in the early Cretaceous. Both of these finds were in areas that have been well searched by dinosaur hunters for over 100 years. These two new dinosaurs share the feature of a sicklelike, slashing claw.

Deinonychus was first found in 1964, and since then more material has surfaced. It was a lightweight animal, only six feet long, with a powerful, high-sided skull, strong, long-fingered hands, and a stiff tail for balancing the animal as it ran. The slashing claw was carried on the second toe from the inside. It was kept folded up when the animal was walking or running, but it could swing straight down when it was needed. *Deinonychus* was clearly agile enough to balance on one leg while slashing with the other, or to leap through the air at its prey. It is likely that *Deinonychus* hunted the large plant-eating ornithopods in packs, as wild dogs do today.

The slashing claw of ▶ Velociraptor *("speedy thief"), a* Deinonychus *relative from China*

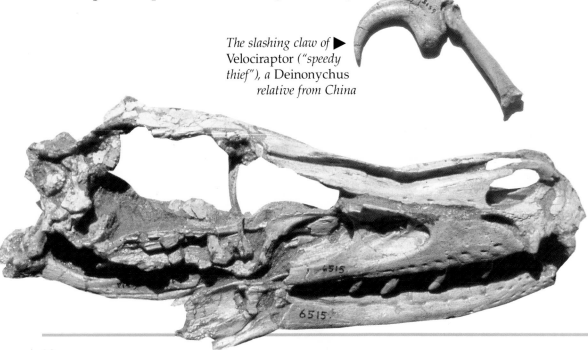

◀ *The skull of* Velociraptor, *showing how lightly built it was. The very few teeth are typical of meat eaters of this period.*

THE CLAW: *Baryonyx* was found by an amateur collector in a brick pit in England in 1983. It had a huge claw that measured 12 inches around the curve, but it is still not clear whether the claw was on the dinosaur's hand or its foot. If it was on the hand, *Baryonyx* was unique among flesh-eating dinosaurs. Fish scales have been found inside the dinosaur, so probably it ate fish. If it did, it could have used its claw to spear its prey. *Baryonyx* was about 30 feet long and had an extremely long, crocodile-shaped skull.

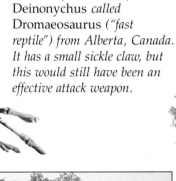

▼ *Reconstructions of some sickle-clawed dinosaurs.* Baryonyx *(top), with its long-snouted skull, was not closely related to the others—Dromaeosaurus (middle right), Deinonychus (bottom left),* and *Velociraptor (bottom right).*

▲ *The great slashing claw of* Baryonyx, *about a foot long, compared with a pair of smaller, more usual claws from other dinosaurs*

◀ *Skeleton of a relative of* Deinonychus *called* Dromaeosaurus *("fast reptile") from Alberta, Canada. It has a small sickle claw, but this would still have been an effective attack weapon.*

▲ *Ockley Quarry in England, where* Baryonyx *was discovered in 1983. The clay is dug up for brickmaking, and bones are often found here.*

The Iguanodontids

I n the early Cretaceous, the most common dinosaurs were the hypsilophodontids and their close relatives, the iguanodontids ("iguana teeth"). The iguanodontids also spread far and wide, to Europe, North America, Africa, Asia, and Australia. There seem to have been huge numbers of them. Single locations have produced dozens of skeletons of animals that lived in herds.

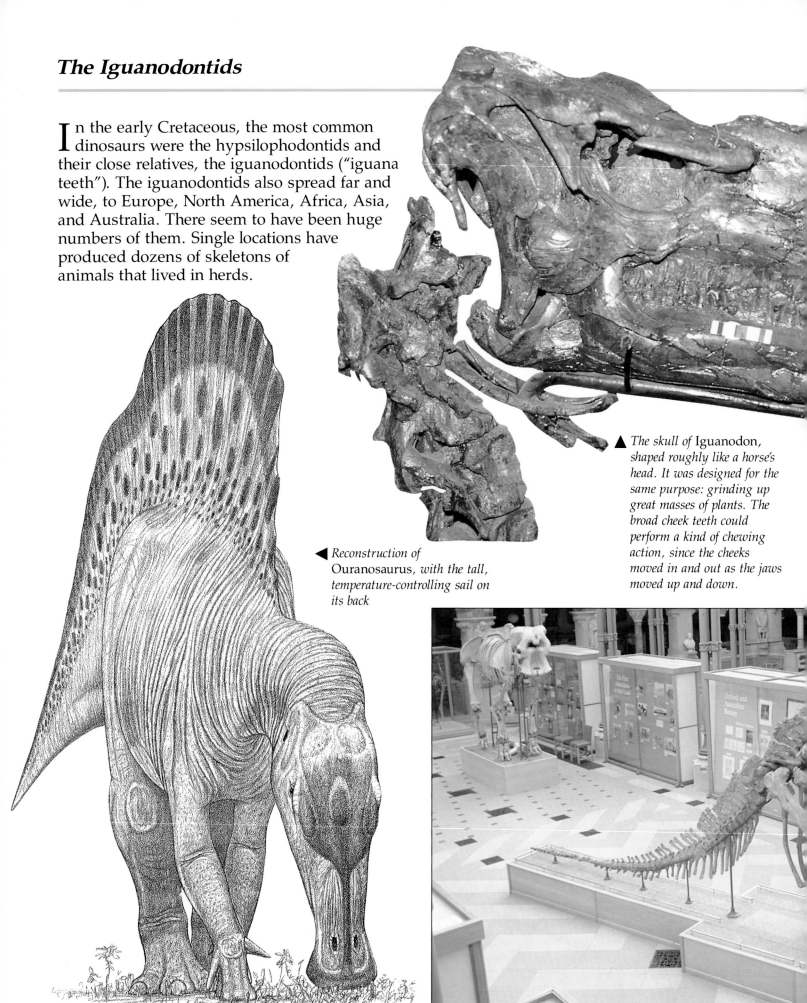

◄ *Reconstruction of* Ouranosaurus, *with the tall, temperature-controlling sail on its back*

▲ *The skull of* Iguanodon, *shaped roughly like a horse's head. It was designed for the same purpose: grinding up great masses of plants. The broad cheek teeth could perform a kind of chewing action, since the cheeks moved in and out as the jaws moved up and down.*

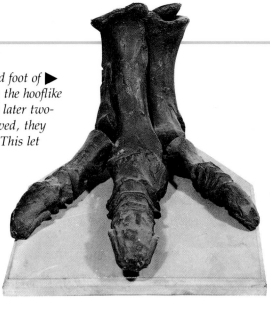

The massive three-toed foot of ▶ Iguanodon, *showing the hooflike ends on the claws. As later two-legged dinosaurs evolved, they lost two of their toes. This let them run faster.*

The hand of Iguanodon. *The* ▶ *three middle fingers had hooves, which tells us that the animal sometimes walked on all fours. The thumb is a single great spike.*

◀ *Skeleton of* Iguanodon. *This kangaroolike pose is probably not the way it would have held itself in life; its tail would have been held up off the ground.*

MYSTERY TEETH: Bones of *Iguanodon* itself were commonly found in southern England in the early 1800s. The species was named in 1825 by a family doctor named Dr. Gideon Mantell. It was only the second dinosaur to be named, after *Megalosaurus*. (Keep in mind that the whole idea of dinosaurs was still very new.) In 1822, Mrs. Mantell found two large teeth on a pile of road-mending stone. Dr. Mantell showed them to every expert he could find. He was told they came from everything from hippopotamuses to lizards. Eventually, he decided it was a giant extinct lizard, since its teeth looked like those of a preserved iguana he found in a museum. Since then, people have been finding *Iguanodons* all over the world, most recently in North America in 1990.

The iguanodontids had the same in-and-out way of chewing as the hypsilophodontids. They were large animals, up to 33 feet. Generally, they walked on two feet, although they could go on all fours. They had hooflike claws on most fingers, and a defensive spiked thumb claw.

BRAVE REPTILE: One relative of *Iguanodon* was *Ouranosaurus* ("brave reptile"), from the Sahara region of Africa. It had a bony "sail" running down its back, which may have been used for temperature control, in the same way that the plates on the back of *Stegosaurus* were.

New Armored Dinosaurs

The stegosaurs were the main form of armored dinosaurs during the Jurassic. As this group declined during the Cretaceous, new types of armored dinosaurs evolved. They had heavier armor and often thicker skulls than the stegosaurs did. These dinosaurs were the ancestors of some familiar dinosaurs of the late Cretaceous (see pages 54–55).

SPINY DINOSAURS: Evidence of two groups of these creatures has been found in the Weald of southern England: the ankylosaurs ("hook-jointed reptiles") and the pachycephalosaurs ("thick-headed reptiles"). Of these two groups, the ankylosaurs were the more common. Skeletons of *Hylaeosaurus* ("wood reptile") and *Polacanthus* ("many spines"), two kinds of ankylosaurs, show that these creatures were 13 feet long and had long spines, or spikes, down the neck and back and on the tail. These dinosaurs were small compared with the dinosaurs of the late Cretaceous.

One the earliest pachycephalosaurs may have been a small, late Cretaceous dinosaur called *Yaverlandia.*All we know about it comes from a small piece of a skull. The skull reveals that the creature must have had bumps on its head.

DINOSAURS WITH BEAKS: A third group of armored dinosaurs, the ceratopsians ("horn-heads"), arose in the early Cretaceous. Scientists have discovered bones of these dinosaurs in Mongolia. What is believed to be the oldest of these creatures, *Psittacosaurus* ("parrot reptile"), looked something like *Hypsilophodon* but had a strange beaked skull and no teeth in the front half of its jaws. *Psittacosaurus* probably used its beak to nip off tough plants.

Partial skeleton of ▶ Psittacosaurus sinensis ("Psittacosaurus from China"), found in Mongolia. The skeleton includes the hip girdle (middle top), ribs, two thigh bones, and a foot.

◀ *Skull of* Yaverlandia bitholus, *the oldest known pachycephalosaur. The bone that covered the top of its head was extremely thick. Scientists believe that the extra bone helped this creature when it got into head-butting fights.*

Complete ▶ skeleton of Psittacosaurus sinensis *from Mongolia, showing the head (left) and the body, including tail, arms, and legs extending to the right*

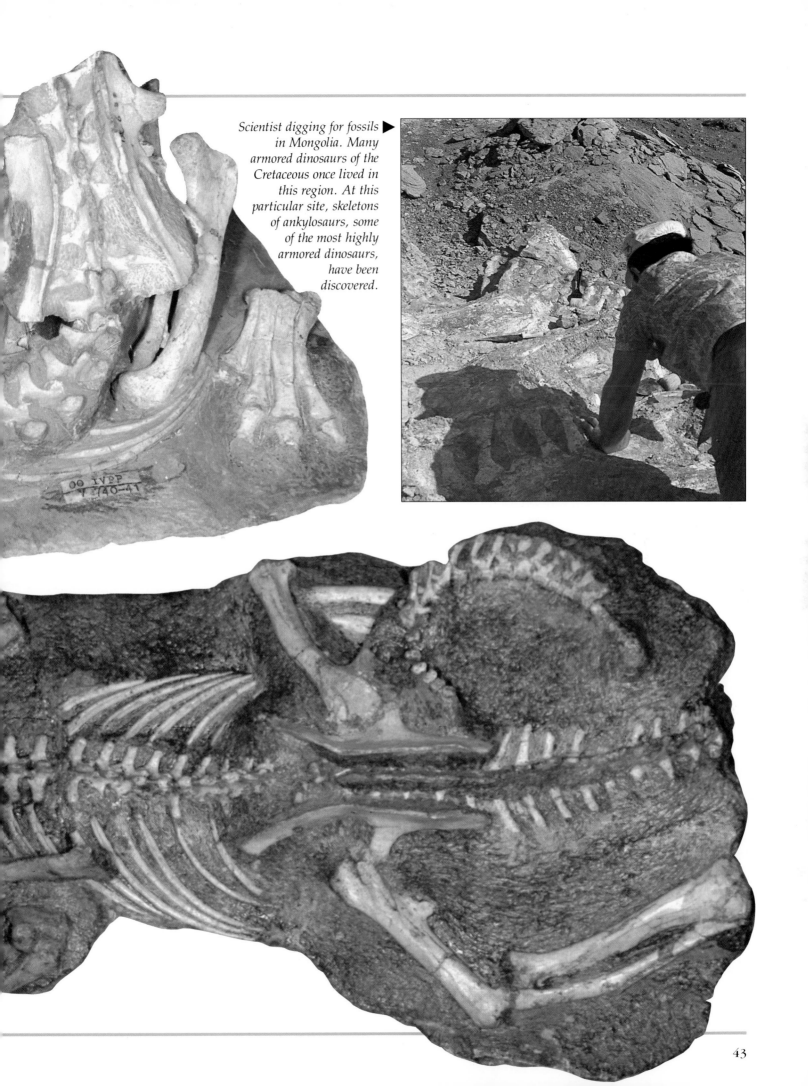

Scientist digging for fossils in Mongolia. Many armored dinosaurs of the Cretaceous once lived in this region. At this particular site, skeletons of ankylosaurs, some of the most highly armored dinosaurs, have been discovered.

5 The Late Cretaceous World

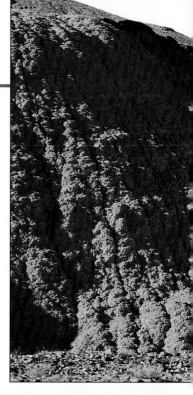

▲ Scientists digging in this barren region of Mongolia have found evidence of dinosaur egg shells and nests of dinosaur eggs from the late Cretaceous period.

Dinosaurs of the late Cretaceous are much better known than dinosaurs of earlier periods. Why? The reason is simple. Bones and fossils from this period have been found all over the world. Also, a greater number of dinosaurs and many more different types of dinosaurs roamed the earth during this time than during any other time in history. Perhaps as many as 20 different species lived side by side in any given region in the world. Before the late Cretaceous period, no more than 10 different species probably lived in the same area.

WHERE THEY LIVED: The places where most late Cretaceous dinosaur remains have been discovered are in North America (especially in Montana and in Alberta, Canada) and in eastern Asia (in Mongolia). In the 1800s, many scientists explored the ancient dry riverbeds of North America for signs of late Cretaceous dinosaurs. There they discovered many of the most famous

▼ In the mud and sands of Alberta, Canada, the bones and fossils of many late Cretaceous dinosaurs have been found. The whole area was once covered by rivers.

In the late Cretaceous, ▶ meat-eating dinosaurs like this Dromaeosaurus and its child would feed on dead creatures such as this horned dinosaur.

▲ *The largest flying reptile in the world,* Quetzalcoatlus *("plumed serpent"), used to soar above these lands in what is now Texas. Its wingspan was 48 feet.*

▼ *A meat-eating* Albertosaurus *("reptile from Alberta") is feeding on the carcass of a plant-eating ceratopsian. Both dinosaurs were common in North America.*

dinosaurs and gave them their names: *Tyrannosaurus, Triceratops, Anatosaurus, Corythosaurus,* and *Ankylosaurus.*

In the 20th century, scientists seeking more information about late Cretaceous dinosaurs began turning their attention to Mongolia. Much to their amazement, when they examined the dinosaur remains they found there, they discovered that the dinosaurs that had once lived in Mongolia matched the dinosaurs found in North America species for species. They were very similar but not quite the same.

PLANT EATERS: In both regions, for example, the main plant eaters were duck-billed ornithopods, horned ceratopsians, armored ankylosaurs, and bone-headed pachycephalosaurs. Meat eaters included the small ostrich dinosaurs, some odd theropods, and the giant tyrannosaurs. Only the sauropods have not been found in both places.

The Ostrich Dinosaurs

Two groups of meat-eating dinosaurs rose to importance in the late Cretaceous: the ornithomimosaurs ("bird-mimics") and the oviraptorosaurs ("egg-stealers"). Both groups had absolutely no teeth. It is hard to understand why meat eaters would have lost their teeth as they evolved. On the other hand, birds like eagles and vultures seem to manage perfectly well today without teeth.

LONG AND FAST: The ornithomimosaurs are known only from North America and Mongolia. They were generally about 10 to 13 feet long, and they were lightweight, since most of their length was tail and neck. *Ornithomimus* was an ostrichlike animal, with a small head like a bird's on a long, flexible neck. It had a rounded body and long, slender legs. Running like an ostrich, with great rapid strides, it may have been able to reach a speed of 40 miles per hour. It had a long tail for balancing and powerful, long-fingered hands. These may have been used for grasping prey or even eggs.

Struthiomimus ("ostrich-mimic") also looked very much like an ostrich. Scientists believe that, like an ostrich, it may have had a very varied diet, including fruits, insects, and small reptiles.

The only oviraptorosaur we know of is *Oviraptor*, found in Mongolia. It may have been a relative of the ornithomimosaurs. *Oviraptor* is also toothless, but the skull is very oddly shaped. It is short and very high, and the lower jaw does not meet the upper jaw for much of its length. There seem to be many different skull shapes, too, some of them having bumps over the nose, others having large crests. The rest of the skeleton is not very well known. A possible North American oviraptorosaur may be *Caenagnathus*, a dinosaur named long ago for its strange lower jaw.

Skeleton of Struthiomimus, ▶ *just as it was found in Canada. The head is bent back because of the drying of the carcass. Like an ostrich, it had a long, flexible neck and a short, stiff body.*

▼ *Skull of the ostrich dinosaur* Struthiomimus, *showing the complete absence of teeth. The skull was lightly built, like a bird's, and the long snout was covered by a bony beak.*

▼ *Skeleton of* Tyrannosaurus rex, *possibly the most famous dinosaur of all. It weighed about six tons, and may have been a scavenger as well as a hunter.*

▲ *Tyrannosaurs on the attack:* Daspletosaurus (left) *and* Tyrannosaurus (middle) *from North America, and* Tarbosaurus (right) *from Mongolia. All had huge heads, long teeth, and powerful three-toed feet for holding down their prey.*

lined with teeth that were up to seven inches long, each one the size of a carving knife. Its open mouth would have been large enough to swallow up a child whole. *Tyrannosaurus* was so large that a fully grown human would have reached only up to its knee. *Tyrannosaurus* could easily have attacked any of the plant eaters of its day.

RELATIVES: The other tyrannosaurs include a nearly identical large form from Mongolia, *Tarbosaurus,* as well as smaller relatives from North America, such as *Albertosaurus* and *Daspletosaurus.* The tyrannosaurs from other parts of the world are still too poorly known to be sure of their appearance and relationships.

The Last Sauropods

The heyday of the sauropods was in the late Jurassic, when these huge four-legged dinosaurs spread all over the world. The sauropods were the most common plant-eating dinosaurs. During the Cretaceous, these creatures began dying out. But some important members of the sauropods thrived, mostly in southern continents.

CRETACEOUS SAUROPODS: Scientists have identified at least two early Cretaceous sauropods, a diplodocid and a brachiosaurid. A diplodocid called *Nemegtosaurus* lived in Mongolia in the late Cretaceous. We know it was a diplodocid because its skull—all that remains of the creature's skeleton—is similar to skulls of *Dipolodocus* from the late Jurassic. A headless skeleton, also found in Mongolia, has been named *Opisthocoelicaudia* ("tail with rear cavity").

AN UNUSUAL TAIL: *Opisthocoelicaudia* had massive, pillarlike legs and an unusual tail that

▼ *A large humerus (upper arm bone) of a sauropod is uncovered from early Cretaceous sediments on the Isle of Wight. These giants were rare in the Cretaceous.*

▲ *A sauropod limb bone in the process of being excavated in England. Such huge bones require as much care as smaller ones, since they can easily break.*

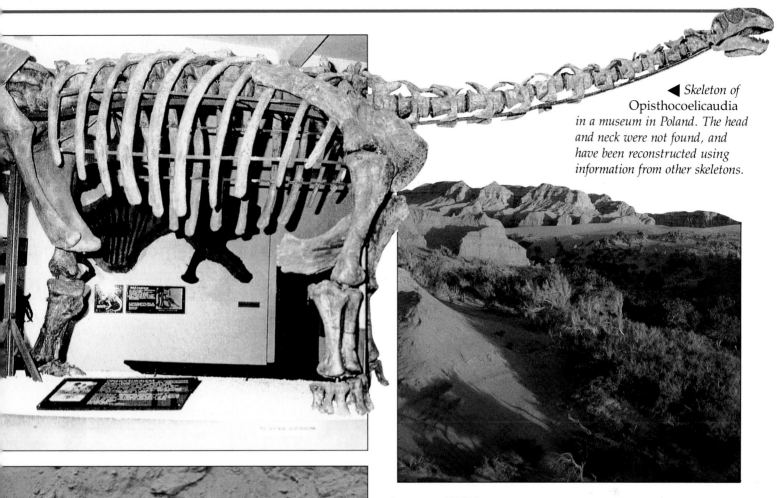

◀ *Skeleton of* Opisthocoelicaudia *in a museum in Poland. The head and neck were not found, and have been reconstructed using information from other skeletons.*

◀ *A team of Polish paleontologists excavates the skeleton of the late Cretaceous sauropod* Opisthocoelicaudia *at Altan Ula, Mongolia, in 1970.*

▲ *The site called Khermeen Tsav in Mongolia. In this area, many dinosaurs have been found by Polish and Russian teams of paleontologists.*

did not bend downward. It actually stuck out backward and a little upward. Scientists think that *Opisthocoelicaudia* used its tail as a kind of "third leg" when it reared up on its hind legs to feed.

During the late Cretaceous, the main sauropods were the titanosaurs, such as *Saltasaurus* ("reptile from Salta," a province in Argentina); *Titanosaurus* ("gigantic reptile"), found in Argentina and India; and *Hypselosaurus*, found in France. It had a long, thin neck and a long, whiplike tail. *Saltasaurus* and *Titanosaurus* were especially interesting because they had similar rounded armor plates set into their skin at the back. The sites in southern France where *Hypselosaurus* has been found have also yielded many fragments of this dinosaur's eggshells.

The Ankylosaurs

Ankylosaurs were heavy, four-legged, armored dinosaurs. They first appeared in the early Cretaceous but became more common in the late Cretaceous. Some, like *Nodosaurus* from North America, resembled their early Cretaceous ancestors, with a covering of armor plates over the back, the tail, and the head, and with a flexible, pointed tail.

WALKING TANKS: A new ankylosaur group began spreading in the late Cretaceous. These dinosaurs had broad, triangular heads that were as wide as they were long. They also sported bony tail clubs. The largest ankylosaurs, *Euoplocephalus* ("well-armored head") and *Ankylosaurus* ("hook-jointed reptile") from North America, and *Talarurus* from Mongolia, were the size and weight of small armored tanks. Their skulls were covered with a "second skull," an outer plating of extra bones that formed in the skin and protected the head. *Euoplocephalus* even had bony eyelid covers to protect its eyes. These ankylosaurs also had horns at the back of the skull.

A NEW WEAPON: The body and tail were covered with rings of bony plates set in the skin, with odd, bony spines scattered here and there. The most amazing feature was the tail club. The last few bones of the tail were fused together to make a rounded double club. The tail in front of the club was flexible. This probably allowed the club to be swung very hard at any predator that was trying to attack.

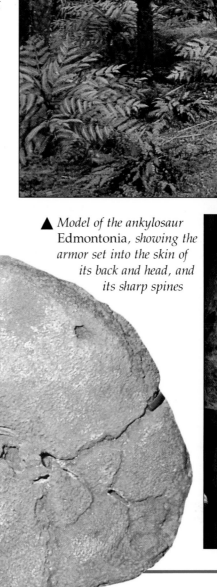

Tail club of Euoplocephalus. ▶ *The tail club is made from a fused mass of bone, including the last tail vertebrae.*

▲ *Model of the ankylosaur* Edmontonia, *showing the armor set into the skin of its back and head, and its sharp spines*

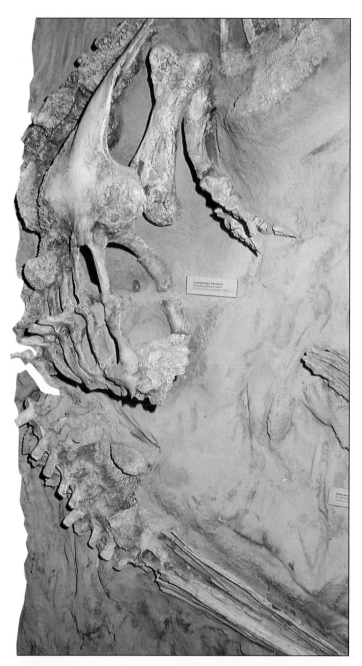

Partial skeleton of the ▶ *ankylosaur* Euoplocephalus, *showing the backbone, hip bones (top left),* hind limb (top right), *and scattered ribs*

Uncovering the ankylosaur ▶ Saichania *in Mongolia. The massive, armored head faces to the right. Excavating dinosaur bones is slow, delicate work done carefully with small tools.*

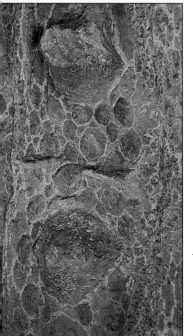

◀ *The preserved skin of* Scolosaurus. *The large and small bumps and plates of bone formed something like the chain mail knights wore beneath their armor.*

The Duckbills

In the late Cretaceous, an amazing group of ornithopods called hadrosaurs, or duck-billed dinosaurs, took the stage. There were dozens of species worldwide, although most have been found in North America and Mongolia. Often, six or seven species lived side by side with one another in any one place.

Most of the duckbills had strange crests on their heads. *Corythosaurus* ("reptile with a Corinthian helmet") had a high crest like a dinner plate; *Parasaurolophus* ("almost a ridged lizard") had a long, snorkel-like structure; and *Tsintaosaurus* ("reptile from Tsintao, China") had a forward-pointing spike. Two other duckbills, *Edmontosaurus* and *Anatosaurus*, had a low, inflated area on top of the snout.

WATER OR LAND? At first, it was thought that duckbills lived in the water, like ducks, and that their crests were like divers' air tanks, for storing air while they dived. But then scientists realized that the duckbills were far too big to be sustained by the amount of air that could be stored in the crest.

HONK! The crest was hollow inside, and breathing tubes passed from the nostrils up through the crest and down the throat. Experiments with models have shown that when a duckbill breathed out, it made a honking or whistling sound through the tubes in the crest. Each crest made a different sound, just as the wind instruments in an orchestra do. Males and females and young duckbills had different crests. We can imagine the late Cretaceous forests reverberating to a din of honks and whistles as babies tried to find their mothers, males and females tried to find mates of the right species, and others made threatening displays!

▼ *Mounted skeleton of the hadrosaur* Lambeosaurus, *lying just as it was preserved in the sediments. The large, flaglike crest points forward, and its size means that this was probably a male.*

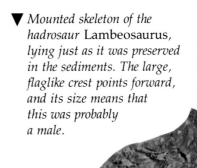

▲ Skull of a crestless dinosaur, Edmontosaurus. *The front of the snout was toothless, but the bony pads there grasped leaves.*

◀ Parasaurolophus, *one of the most striking hadrosaurs, with its tubelike head crest. One can see why many thought the crest was a snorkel. But it has no hole at the end, and could not have been used in that way.*

▲ Some hadrosaurs: Lambeosaurus (bottom left) *and* Corythosaurus (bottom right), *and the heads of* Hadrosaurus (top left), Tsintaosaurus (top middle), Parasaurolophus (top right), Edmontosaurus (middle left), *and* Saurolophus (middle)

◀ A nesting place of the hadrosaur Maiasaura *in Montana. Two parents are tending their newly hatched young, still in the nest.*

▲ Skull of Corythosaurus. *It has a rounded, platelike crest made from the bones on top of the snout, which grew up and back.*

57

The Boneheads

If you had been able to see a real pachycephalosaur, you might have thought it was a very smart dinosaur. Such a large head, you might reason, must have held a very large brain. But, in fact, all it held was a lot of bone. The oddest feature of this group of dinosaurs is the enormously thickened skull roof they all shared. In some species, it amounted to ten inches of solid bone! This characteristic is what gave rise to their name. Pachycephalosaur means "thick-headed reptile." For most of these animals, scientists have not much more fossil evidence to go on than a thickened head shield. Few are known from more complete remains.

DOME-HEADS: Two pachycephalosaurs were found earlier this century in Montana and Alberta: *Stegoceras* ("horned roof"), which was only 6.5 feet long, and the larger *Pachycephalosaurus*, which was 26 feet long. At first, only bits and pieces of their skulls were found, but afterward one or two skeletons also surfaced. These showed that the pachycephalosaurs walked on two legs and had a raised dome on the head. In *Stegoceras*, the dome was high and rose over the whole snout; *Pachycephalosaurus*'s dome rose over the back half of the skull, which also had bony spines behind and on the snout.

NO BUTTS: More recent finds from Mongolia have shown that the pachycephalosaurs had extra-strong hip bones, backbones, and bones in the neck. These features, and the thick skull, were a mystery until someone suggested that perhaps these dinosaurs head-butted one another. They may have been establishing dominance over territory or attracting mates, just as wild sheep and goats do today. The thickened skull roof protected the brain (small as it was) against enormous impact as the animals clashed. The force of the blow then traveled down the neck to be finally absorbed in the hip region.

Skull of Pachycephalosaurus, *one of the best-known bone-headed dinosaurs. The knobbly spines may have been for protection or to look attractive to mates. The massively thickened skull roof is above the eye socket.*

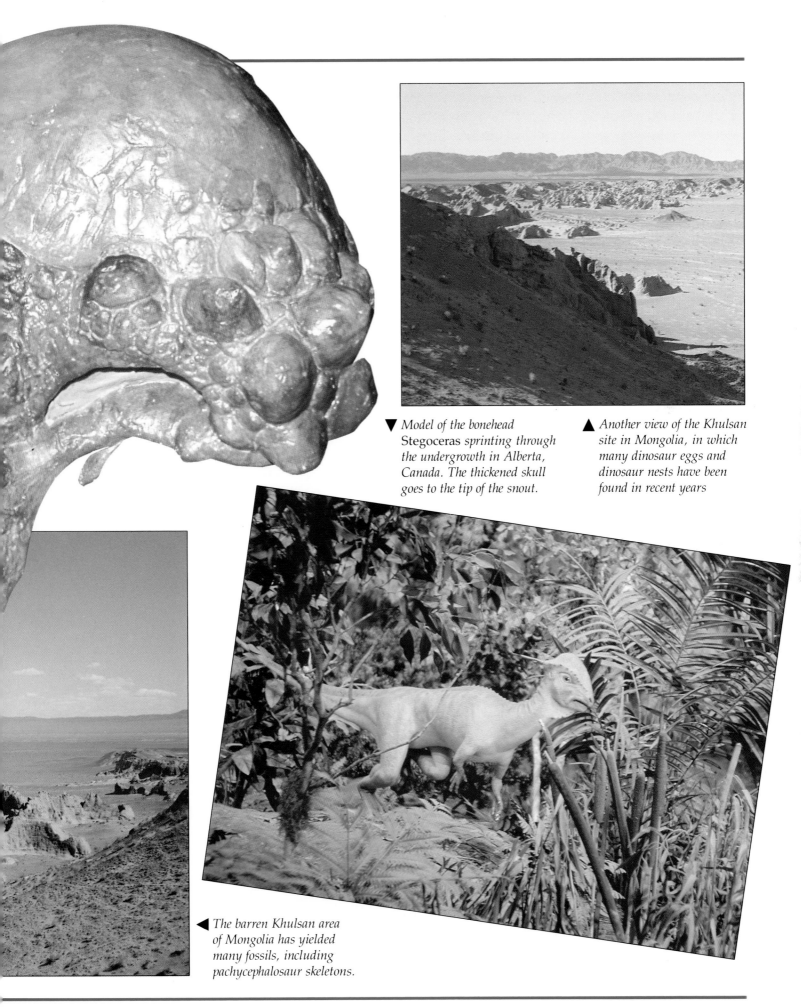

▼ Model of the bonehead
Stegoceras *sprinting through
the undergrowth in Alberta,
Canada. The thickened skull
goes to the tip of the snout.*

▲ Another view of the Khulsan
site in Mongolia, in which
many dinosaur eggs and
dinosaur nests have been
found in recent years

◄ *The barren Khulsan area
of Mongolia has yielded
many fossils, including
pachycephalosaur skeletons.*

The Horned Dinosaurs

The ceratopsians, or horned dinosaurs, were close relatives of the boneheads. They were nearly as common as the duckbills in the late Cretaceous. The earliest ceratopsian was the two-legged *Psittacosaurus* (see page 42), but these dinosaurs soon became four-legged, like *Protoceratops* ("early horn-head"). This small animal, six feet long, was found in Mongolia in the 1920s, by an expedition from the American Museum of Natural History. *Protoceratops* had a beaked snout, a shield of bone over its neck, and a thickened area on top of its snout. Its eggs were laid in circles of 10 or 20, and buried in warm sand. Some of the nests found by the expedition even had babies near them.

COLLARED: As ceratopsians evolved into different species, each of them had a neck frill, which was a bit like a large, ruffed collar. This was an outgrowth of the bones around the back of the skull. The frills took on all kinds of shapes: in *Triceratops* ("three-horned head"), the edge was covered with bony bumps; in *Styracosaurus* ("spiked reptile"), there were several long, scary spikes; in *Torosaurus*, the frill made the skull very long. One specimen of *Torosaurus*, in fact, is 25 feet long altogether, and its skull is 8.5 feet long.

This is the all-time largest head of any land animal.

Each ceratopsian also had a nose horn like a present-day rhinoceros's, and they sometimes had other facial horns, as well. *Protoceratops* had a raised area on the snout, but all the later forms had long nose horns. *Triceratops* and *Torosaurus* also had a long horn over each eye.

GOOD DEFENSE: The neck frill would have protected the neck from attack, and it was also a place for the jaw muscles to attach. The horns on the face must have been useful in defense, too. It is possible that herds of ceratopsians would form a circle around their young, heads and horns facing out, to keep any *Tyrannosaurus* from coming too close.

Skeleton of Triceratops ▶ horridus *("horrible Triceratops"), showing its three horns, one on the snout and a long one over each eye socket. The broad hands and feet have hooves instead of claws, and the limb structure tells us that this large ceratopsian could gallop fast.*

▼ *Model of baby* Protoceratops *hatching from their eggs. Many eggs, nests, and babies of this species have been found.*

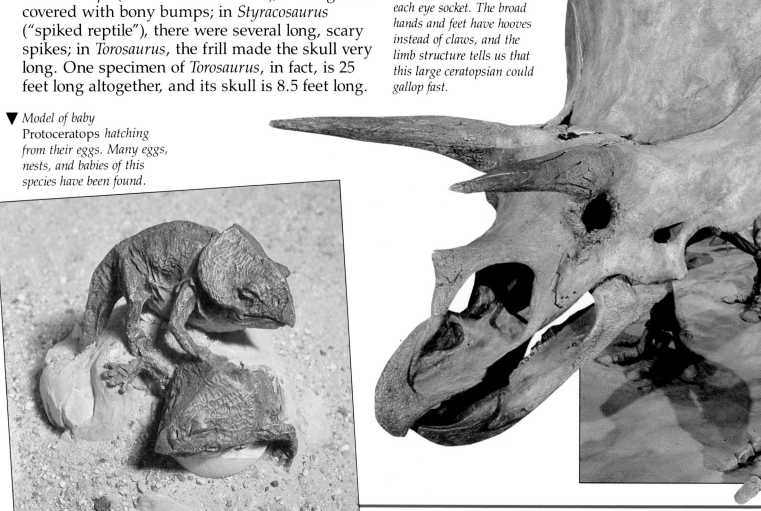

▲ *Skull of the early ceratopsian* Protoceratops. *It has a neck frill but no horn on its snout, just a bone thickening.*

Typical ceratopsians: ▶
Torosaurus (top left),
Styracosaurus (top right),
Triceratops (bottom left),
Centrosaurus (bottom right),
and Protoceratops (middle).

▼ *Skeleton of* Chasmosaurus, *a ceratopsian from Alberta, Canada. The neck frill was very long, and the weight of* the head very massive; this animal needed powerful neck muscles.

Why Did They Die Out?

The last dinosaurs disappeared 65 million years ago. For a long time, the explanation seemed simple. The dinosaurs had been around for long enough, and they were huge, lumbering monsters that were not clever enough to survive. They just died off in the face of competition from the hairy, warm-blooded mammals that were to replace them.

Scientists have been having second thoughts, however. For one thing, the dinosaurs were thriving, especially in the late Cretaceous. In fact, they had never been so varied and so plentiful. For another, there is no sign of decline over a long period; they lived right up to the end, with the last-gasp dinosaurs being very successful species like *Triceratops*, *Tyrannosaurus*, and many duckbills.

COLD? There are now two general theories for what happened. One is that climates became cooler, and the dinosaurs dwindled away over several million years as their warm habitats disappeared. This long-term kind of view can also explain the mass extinction of other animals at the same time. The flying pterosaurs disappeared about then, as did the great sea reptiles and many other sea creatures.

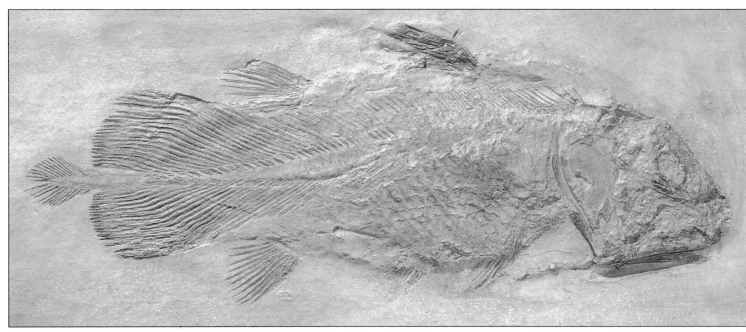

◀ *Skeleton of an ichthyosaur, one of a dolphinlike sea reptile group that died out in the late Cretaceous, but sometime before the dinosaurs died out.*

▼ *Underside of the shell of a prehistoric turtle. The bony undershell that protects the body is visible, as well as a partial limb. The turtles seemed to survive the mass extinction that wiped out the dinosaurs 65 million years ago.*

DISASTER? The other theory is that there was a great disaster. An asteroid, or tiny planet, may have hit the earth and sent a vast cloud of shattered rocks and dust high into the atmosphere, where it circled the earth, blacked out the sun, and caused a long spell of darkness and great cold. Many plants and animals on land and in the seas would have perished, and these victims would have included the dinosaurs.

WHICH THEORY? At the moment, it is hard to decide between these theories. However, one of the real mysteries is why so many animals survived. Fishes, frogs, turtles, lizards, crocodiles, birds, and mammals all lived on. No theory can yet explain why they survived and the dinosaurs and others disappeared.

▼ *The shell of a modern-day giant land tortoise. Turtles are the oldest reptiles still alive; they were already on earth during the Triassic, at the time of the earliest dinosaurs. Those earliest turtles could not retract their necks. Today's turtles have changed very little from the earliest ones.*

▲ *Model of the giant pterosaur* Pteranodon, *one of the last survivors of its group. The pterosaurs ruled the skies for 160 million years, the same span of time the dinosaurs did, but they were eventually replaced by birds.*

◀ *The coelacanth* Holophagus penicillata, *from the Jurassic. At one time, it was thought that these unusual fishes had died out during the Jurassic or Cretaceous, until a living coelacanth,* Latimeria, *was fished up off the east coast of Africa in 1938.*

Further Reading about Dinosaurs

Benton, Michael. *The Dinosaur Encyclopedia*. New York: Simon and Schuster, 1984.

Dixon, Dougal. *The Illustrated Dinosaur Encyclopedia*. New York: Smithmark Publishers Inc., 1991.

Norman, David. *Dinosaur*. New York: Prentice Hall, 1991.

————.*The Prehistoric World of the Dinosaur*. New York: Gallery Books, 1988.

Sattler, Helen Roney. *The New Illustrated Dinosaur Dictionary*. New York: Lothrop, Lee & Shepard, 1990.

Picture Credits

Index